First World War
and Army of Occupation
War Diary
France, Belgium and Germany

18 DIVISION
Divisional Troops
92 Field Company Royal Engineers
27 July 1915 - 3 August 1919

WO95/2027/3

The Naval & Military Press Ltd
www.nmarchive.com
Published in association with The National Archives

Published by

The Naval & Military Press Ltd

Unit 10 Ridgewood Industrial Park,

Uckfield, East Sussex,

TN22 5QE England

Tel: +44 (0) 1825 749494

www.naval-military-press.com

www.nmarchive.com

This diary has been reprinted in facsimile from the original. Any imperfections are inevitably reproduced and the quality may fall short of modern type and cartographic standards.

© **Crown Copyright**
Images reproduced by permission of The National Archives, London, England, 2015.

Contents

Document type	Place/Title	Date From	Date To
Heading	WO95/2027/3		
Heading	18th Division 92nd Field Coy R.E. Sep 1915 Aug 1919		
Heading	18th Division 92nd F.C. R.E. Vol I July & Aug 15		
Heading	War Diary of 92 Field Co R.E. from 27.7.15 to 31.8.15.		
War Diary	Southampton	27/07/1915	27/07/1915
War Diary	Havre	28/07/1915	29/07/1915
War Diary	Coisy	30/07/1915	05/08/1915
War Diary	Millencourt	06/08/1915	31/08/1915
Heading	18th Division 92nd F.C. R.E. Vol 2 Sep 15 Aug 19		
Heading	War Diary of 92nd Field Co. R.E. from 1-9-15 to 30-9-15.		
War Diary	Millencourt	01/09/1915	20/09/1915
War Diary	Dernancourt	20/09/1915	30/09/1915
Heading	18th Division 92nd F.C. R.E. Vol 3 Oct 15		
Heading	War Diary of 92nd Field Co. R.E. from 1-10-15 to 31-10-15		
War Diary	Dernancourt	01/10/1915	31/10/1915
War Diary		19/10/1915	31/10/1915
Heading	18th Division 92nd F.C. R.E. Vol I Nov 15 121/7624		
Heading	92nd Field Coy R.E. Diary from 1.11.15. to 30.11.15.		
War Diary	Dernancourt	01/11/1915	06/11/1915
War Diary	Dernancourt	01/11/1915	30/11/1915
War Diary	Dernancourt	07/11/1915	20/11/1915
War Diary	Dernancourt	01/11/1915	30/11/1915
Heading	18th Div 92nd F.C. R.E. Vol: 5		
Heading	War Diary of 92nd Field Co. R.E. from 1.12.15. to 31.12.15		
War Diary	Dernancourt	01/12/1915	05/12/1915
War Diary	Dernancourt	01/12/1915	31/12/1915
War Diary	Dernancourt	28/12/1915	28/12/1915
Heading	92nd F.C. R.E. Vol: 6 Jan		
Heading	War Diary of 92nd Field Co. R.E. from 1-1-16 to 31-1-16.		
War Diary	Dernancourt	01/01/1916	31/01/1916
War Diary		06/01/1916	16/01/1916
War Diary		08/01/1916	12/01/1916
Heading	War Diary of 92nd Field Company R.E. from 1st February to 29th February 1916.		
War Diary	Dernancourt	01/02/1916	29/02/1916
War Diary	Dernancourt	16/02/1916	16/02/1916
War Diary	Dernancourt	08/02/1916	08/02/1916
War Diary	Dernancourt	31/01/1916	23/02/1916
War Diary	Dernancourt	08/02/1916	17/02/1916
Heading	War Diary of 92nd Field Company R.E. from 1.3.16 to 31.3.16.		
War Diary	Frechencourt	01/03/1916	21/03/1916
War Diary	Bray & Suzanne	21/03/1916	31/03/1916
War Diary	Bray	01/03/1916	31/03/1916
Heading	War Diary of 92nd Field Co. R.E. from 1/4/16 to 30/4/16.		

War Diary	Bray and Suzanne	01/04/1916	30/04/1916
War Diary	Bray	01/04/1916	30/04/1916
War Diary		01/04/1916	29/04/1916
War Diary		14/04/1916	24/04/1916
War Diary	Bray	01/05/1916	07/05/1916
War Diary		06/05/1916	14/05/1916
War Diary	Bray	08/05/1916	28/05/1916
War Diary	Bray	15/05/1916	31/05/1916
War Diary	Bray	01/05/1916	31/05/1916
War Diary		01/05/1916	29/05/1916
War Diary	Burbure	01/05/1916	07/05/1916
War Diary	Maroc	08/05/1916	18/05/1916
War Diary	Burbure	19/05/1916	25/05/1916
War Diary	Coyecque	26/05/1916	27/05/1916
War Diary	Burbure	28/05/1916	31/05/1916
Heading	War Diary of 92nd Field Company RE from 1-6-16 to 30-6-16.		
War Diary	Bray	01/06/1916	14/06/1916
War Diary	Bray	08/06/1916	30/06/1916
War Diary	Bray	01/06/1916	30/06/1916
Heading	92nd Field Company R.E. Vol 12		
Heading	Headquarters 18 Division.	04/08/1916	04/08/1916
War Diary	Carnoy	01/07/1916	05/07/1916
War Diary	Bray	06/07/1916	12/07/1916
War Diary	Copse Valley	13/07/1916	13/07/1916
War Diary	Bray	15/07/1916	21/07/1916
War Diary	Hocqincourt	22/07/1916	24/07/1916
War Diary	Staple	25/07/1916	28/07/1916
War Diary	St Jan Cappel	29/07/1916	01/08/1916
War Diary		01/07/1916	31/07/1916
War Diary	St Jan Cappel	01/08/1916	14/08/1916
War Diary	Bois Grenier	14/08/1916	14/08/1916
War Diary	Culvert Farm	14/08/1916	14/08/1916
War Diary	Jocks Joy.	14/08/1916	14/08/1916
War Diary	Erquinghem.	14/08/1916	14/08/1916
War Diary	Bois Grenier.	15/08/1916	21/08/1916
War Diary	Jocks Joy.	21/08/1916	21/08/1916
War Diary	Shaftesbury Amm.	21/08/1916	21/08/1916
War Diary	Birdcage.	21/08/1916	21/08/1916
War Diary	B.G. Line.	21/08/1916	21/08/1916
War Diary	Trench 57-58.	21/08/1916	21/08/1916
War Diary	Tramway Avenue	21/08/1916	22/08/1916
War Diary	Estaires.	23/08/1916	25/08/1916
War Diary	Rocourt.	26/08/1916	31/08/1916
War Diary		01/08/1916	31/08/1916
War Diary	Rocourt.	01/09/1916	11/09/1916
War Diary	Pochevillers.	12/09/1916	18/09/1916
War Diary	Acheux Sta.	19/09/1916	21/09/1916
War Diary	Varennes Timber Park.	22/09/1916	24/09/1916
War Diary	Acheux Sta.	19/09/1916	24/09/1916
War Diary	Acheux.	24/09/1916	24/09/1916
War Diary	Acheux.	19/09/1916	24/09/1916
War Diary	Varennes Timber Park.	25/09/1916	29/09/1916
War Diary	Acheux Sta	29/09/1916	29/09/1916
War Diary	Acheux.	29/09/1916	30/09/1916
War Diary	Rocourt.	02/09/1916	09/09/1916

War Diary	Purhevillen.	16/09/1916	16/09/1916
War Diary	Purhevillen.	14/09/1916	14/09/1916
War Diary	Achense.	20/09/1916	04/10/1916
War Diary	Lancashire Dump.	01/10/1916	02/10/1916
War Diary	Schwaben Redoubt.	03/10/1916	10/10/1916
War Diary	Hem.	11/10/1916	15/10/1916
War Diary	Candas.	15/10/1916	15/10/1916
War Diary	Fienvillers.	15/10/1916	18/10/1916
War Diary	Usna Redoubt.	19/10/1916	19/10/1916
War Diary	Tara Hill	19/10/1916	23/10/1916
War Diary	Usna Redoubt.	23/10/1916	23/10/1916
War Diary	Hessian Trench.	21/10/1916	24/10/1916
War Diary	Albert.	22/10/1916	29/10/1916
War Diary		23/10/1916	23/10/1916
War Diary	R.22.27.28.33.34, Tranch Map 57 D.S.E.	24/10/1916	31/10/1916
War Diary	X.14.b.3.9.	30/10/1916	30/10/1916
War Diary	Kay Dump Q.34.c.21.	20/10/1916	31/10/1916
War Diary	Albert.	30/10/1916	30/10/1916
War Diary	Martenpart.	02/10/1916	05/10/1916
War Diary	Aushense Hem.	08/10/1916	15/10/1916
War Diary	Usna Redoubt.	22/10/1916	22/10/1916
War Diary	Albert.	25/10/1916	25/10/1916
War Diary	Mouquet Farm.	01/11/1916	10/11/1916
War Diary	Stuff Redoubt.	10/11/1916	10/11/1916
War Diary	Mouquet Farm.	10/11/1916	10/11/1916
War Diary	X.13.b.28.	01/11/1916	23/11/1916
War Diary	Mouquet Farm.	11/11/1916	23/11/1916
War Diary	Fabeck.	23/11/1916	23/11/1916
War Diary	Zollern Redoubt.	23/11/1916	23/11/1916
War Diary	Field Trench	23/11/1916	23/11/1916
War Diary	Disire Trench.	23/11/1916	27/11/1916
War Diary	X.13.b.28.	11/11/1916	23/11/1916
War Diary	X.I.D.10.	24/11/1916	30/11/1916
War Diary	Mouquet Farm.	08/11/1916	10/11/1916
War Diary		09/11/1916	20/11/1916
War Diary		13/11/1916	15/11/1916
War Diary		13/11/1916	13/11/1916
War Diary	Albert.	01/12/1916	01/12/1916
War Diary	Ovillers.	02/12/1916	21/12/1916
War Diary	Nouvion-En-Ponthieu.	22/12/1916	12/01/1917
War Diary	Outre Bois.	13/01/1917	14/01/1917
War Diary	Beauquesne.	15/01/1917	16/01/1917
War Diary	Mioland Huts W.9.b.9.5.	17/01/1917	18/01/1917
War Diary	W.9.b.9.5.	19/01/1917	21/01/1917
War Diary	N of Buzincourt W.3.0.17 Aueluy Wood A.T.N. Dump W.11.D.8.2. W.11.D.5.7. W.10.C.18. W.9.C.9.5.	21/01/1917	22/01/1917
War Diary	N of Buzincourt	22/01/1917	22/01/1917
War Diary	W.3.c.17 Avelury Wood A.T.N. Dump W.11.D.8.2. W.11.D.5.7. W.10.C.1.8. W.9.b.9.5.	22/01/1917	23/01/1917
War Diary	N of Bouyencourt W.3.c.17 Avelury Wood A.T.N. Dump W.11.D.8.2. W.11.D.5.7. W.10.C.1.8. W.9.b.9.5.	23/01/1917	24/01/1917
War Diary	Ata Dump.	24/01/1917	25/01/1917
War Diary	Div. H.Q.	26/01/1917	26/01/1917
War Diary	Martinsartwood.	26/01/1917	26/01/1917
War Diary	Aveluywood.	28/01/1917	28/01/1917

War Diary	Aveluysioing	28/01/1917	31/01/1917
War Diary	X.2.c.4.8.	01/02/1917	01/02/1917
War Diary	Martinsartwood.	01/02/1917	01/02/1917
War Diary	W.12.D.8.8. W.9.O.9.9. W.12.C.9.3.	01/02/1917	01/02/1917
War Diary	Hedauville.	01/02/1917	01/02/1917
War Diary	W.7.B.	01/02/1917	01/02/1917
War Diary	W.17.A.4.9.	01/02/1917	01/02/1917
War Diary	R.28.b.38.	02/02/1917	03/02/1917
War Diary	V.11.d.8.8.	03/02/1917	03/02/1917
War Diary	Div 1 Q W.C.17. R.2.8.b.3.8. W.11.C.3.0.	04/02/1917	04/02/1917
War Diary	Forceville.	04/02/1917	04/02/1917
War Diary	Hedauville.	04/02/1917	04/02/1917
War Diary	V.11.d.8.8. W.9.d.9.7. W.12.d.7.6.	04/02/1917	04/02/1917
War Diary	Martinsart Verennes.	04/02/1917	04/02/1917
War Diary	Div H.Q. R.28.b.3.8. W.11.c.30.	05/02/1917	05/02/1917
War Diary	Forceville	05/02/1917	05/02/1917
War Diary	Hedauville.	05/02/1917	05/02/1917
War Diary	V.11.d.8.8. W.9.d.9.7. W.12.d.7.6.	05/02/1917	05/02/1917
War Diary	Martinsart Verennes.	05/02/1917	05/02/1917
War Diary	Div H.Q. R.28.b.38. W.11.c.30.	06/02/1917	06/02/1917
War Diary	Forceville.	06/02/1917	06/02/1917
War Diary	Hedauville.	06/02/1917	06/02/1917
War Diary	V.11.d.8.8. W.9.d.9.7. W.12.d.7.6.	06/02/1917	06/02/1917
War Diary	Martinsart Verennes.	06/02/1917	06/02/1917
War Diary	Mailly Maillet.	06/02/1917	06/02/1917
War Diary	Div. H.Q. R.28.b.38. W.11.C.30.	07/02/1917	07/02/1917
War Diary	Forceville	07/02/1917	07/02/1917
War Diary	Hedauville.	07/02/1917	07/02/1917
War Diary	V.11.d.5.8. W.9.d.9.7. W.12.d.7.6.	07/02/1917	07/02/1917
War Diary	Martinsart.	07/02/1917	07/02/1917
War Diary	Mailly Maillet.	07/02/1917	07/02/1917
War Diary	Div. H.Q. R.28.b.30.	08/02/1917	08/02/1917
War Diary	R.28.b.30.	08/02/1917	08/02/1917
War Diary	R.22.b.4.1. R.32.b.87. W.11.c.3.0. V.11.d.8.8. W.9.d.9.7. W.12.d.7.6.	08/02/1917	08/02/1917
War Diary	Headuville.	08/02/1917	08/02/1917
War Diary	Forceville.	08/02/1917	08/02/1917
War Diary	Mailly Maillet.	08/02/1917	08/02/1917
War Diary	Div. H.Q. R.28.b.88. R.22.d.4.1. R.32.b.8.7. W.11.c.3.0. V.11.d.88. W.9.d.97.	09/02/1917	09/02/1917
War Diary	W.12.a.7.6.	09/02/1917	09/02/1917
War Diary	Headuville.	09/02/1917	09/02/1917
War Diary	Forceville.	09/02/1917	09/02/1917
War Diary	Div H.Q. R.28.b.88. R.22.d.4.1. R.32.b.8.7. W.11.c.30. V.11.d.88. W.9.d.9.7. W. 12.d.7.6.	10/02/1917	10/02/1917
War Diary	Hedauville Forceville.	10/02/1917	10/02/1917
War Diary	Div H.Q. R.28.b.88. R.22.b.87. R.32.d.4.1. R.32.b.4.1. R32.b.8.7. R.32.b.9.8. W.11.c.3.0. V.11.d.88. W.9.d.9.7. W.12.d.7.6 Hedauville.	11/02/1917	12/02/1917
War Diary	W.9.9.5.	12/02/1917	12/02/1917
War Diary	St. Pierre Divion	13/02/1917	13/02/1917
War Diary	R.28.b.88. R.22.d.4.1. R.27.d. W.11.c.30.	13/02/1917	13/02/1917
War Diary	Div H.Q. W.12.d.7.6.	13/02/1917	13/02/1917
War Diary	Hedauville.	13/02/1917	13/02/1917
War Diary	X.7.a.4.7.	13/02/1917	13/02/1917
War Diary	Stpierre Divion R.22.d.4.1. R.27.d.	14/02/1917	14/02/1917

War Diary	W.11.c.30. Div H.Q. Hedauville X.7.a.47.	14/02/1917	14/02/1917
War Diary	R.1.3. R.22.d.4.1. R.27.d. W.11.c.3.0.	15/02/1917	15/02/1917
War Diary	Div H.Q. Hedauville X.7.a.4.7. R.32.b.8.9 W.12.d.24. R.8.d.41.	15/02/1917	15/02/1917
War Diary	R.13. R.22.d.41. R.28.a. R.28.a.97. R.3.4.a.	16/02/1917	16/02/1917
War Diary	W.11.c.30. R.12.d.20. R.28.c.72. Div H.Q. R.8.d.2.1.	16/02/1917	16/02/1917
War Diary	R.13.	17/02/1917	17/02/1917
War Diary	Nabjunction to R.22.d.4.1. R.8.d.2.1.	17/02/1917	17/02/1917
War Diary	Stuffredoubt.	17/02/1917	17/02/1917
War Diary	Div H.Q. W.11.c.3.0. R.12.d.20. R.28.C.7.2.	17/02/1917	17/02/1917
War Diary	R.13.	18/02/1917	18/02/1917
War Diary	Nabjunction to R.22.d.4.1.	18/02/1917	18/02/1917
War Diary	Stuffredoubt R.22.6. W.11.c.30. R.12d.20. R.28.d.72. Div H.Q.W.9.d.9.7.	18/02/1917	18/02/1917
War Diary	R.13.	19/02/1917	19/02/1917
War Diary	Nabjunction to R.22.d.4.1.	19/02/1917	19/02/1917
War Diary	R.22.b.7.2. R.16.d.5.7.	19/02/1917	19/02/1917
War Diary	W.11.c.30. R.12.d.20. R.28.c.72. Div H,Q.R13	19/02/1917	19/02/1917
War Diary	R.1.3.	19/02/1917	19/02/1917
War Diary	R.3.2.b.7.7. R.2.2.b.5.3. R.22.b.	20/02/1917	20/02/1917
War Diary	W.11.c.3.0. R.12.d.20. R.28.c.72. Div H.Q. W.9.d.9.7.	20/02/1917	21/02/1917
War Diary	R.22.d.4.1. to R.17.c.2.9.	22/02/1917	22/02/1917
War Diary	R.23.a. R.22.a. R.13.a. W.11.c.3.0. R.12.d.20. Div H.Q. R.10.d. R.17.a.	22/02/1917	23/02/1917
War Diary	R.22.d.41. R.17.c.24. Div H.q. Pup Dump	23/02/1917	23/02/1917
War Diary	R.17.d.20. R.22.d.88. R.22.d.66. R.2.2c.5.2.	24/02/1917	24/02/1917
War Diary	R.22d. R.17.c. R.17.b. R.17.d.20. Pup Dump	26/02/1917	26/02/1917
War Diary	R.22.d. R.17.c. R.17.b. R.5.a.55. R.52a.18. R.5.e.33.	27/02/1917	27/02/1917
War Diary	R.22.d. R.17.b. R.11.c. R.5.c.33. R.5.e.21. R.5.a.55. R.5.a.18.	28/02/1917	28/02/1917
War Diary	2.2.G.H.	01/02/1917	27/02/1917
War Diary	X.2.a.14. R.22.d.47. R.5.c.3.3. W.9.b.9.5.	01/03/1917	01/03/1917
War Diary	Hessian Dump Borm Ravine R.22.d.d7. R.10.b. R.5.c.	01/03/1917	12/03/1917
War Diary	R.5.c.10-45 R.5.c.33.	01/03/1917	12/03/1917
War Diary	R.22.d.41. R.11.c.53. 1.11.c.30.	01/03/1917	12/03/1917
War Diary	L35.c.83-L35.d.33. R.5.c.33. R.11.c78. R.5.c.10-45 R	03/03/1917	05/03/1917
War Diary	R.22.d.41. R.11.c.53. R.b.11.c.30.	05/03/1917	05/03/1917
War Diary	R.5.c.33.	05/03/1917	05/03/1917
War Diary	R.5.a.55-L35.d.33. R.5.c.33. R.11a.78	06/03/1917	06/03/1917
War Diary	R.5.c.10.-45. R.22.d.41. R.11.c.53. R.33.d.53. R.33.b.55.	06/03/1917	06/03/1917
War Diary	X.7. W.11.c.30. W.11.c.30.	06/03/1917	07/03/1917
War Diary	L.35.c.60. L.35.d.33. R5.c.10. R.5.c.45.	08/03/1917	08/03/1917
War Diary	St Pierre Divion.	08/03/1917	08/03/1917
War Diary	L.35.c.95.25. R.5.d.18. R.5.c.3. R.5.c.66. R.11.a.78.	08/03/1917	08/03/1917
War Diary	R.22.d.41. R.11.c.53. R.53.d.53. R.33.b.55.	08/03/1917	08/03/1917
War Diary	L.35.c.52. R.5.c.10. R.5.c.45. L.35.c.95.25. R.5.d.18.	09/03/1917	09/03/1917
War Diary	R.5.c.33. R.5.c.88. R.22.d.41. R.11.c.53. R.3.d.83. A.33.b.58. W.11.c.30.	09/03/1917	09/03/1917
War Diary	R.22.d.41 R.11.c.53. L.35.c.92. L.36.c.0.7. R.5.d.15. R.5.d.57. G.25.b.90.11. W.11.c.3.0.	10/03/1917	10/03/1917
War Diary	R.22.d.42. R.11.c.53. R.5.c.33. R.5.d.87. R.5.c.10. R.5.c.45. R.5.c.87. R.5.a.72. R.5.25.b90.15. W.11.c.30.	11/03/1917	11/03/1917
War Diary	Aabjunction R.11.c.5.3. R.5.c.33. R.5.d.87. R.5.c.10. R.5.c.45. R.5.a.72. W.11.c.30.	12/03/1917	12/03/1917
War Diary	Nabjunction R.11.c.5.3. R.5.c.10. R.5.a.4.6.	13/03/1917	13/03/1917

War Diary	R.5.c.33. R.5.d.87. L.35.d.45. G.31.b.0.0. G.31.b.0.0. 9.31.b.9.6.W.11.c.30.	13/03/1917	13/03/1917
War Diary	Nabjunction R.11.c.5.9. R.5.a.46. L.35.c.45. G.31.b.0.0. R.5.a.7.2.	14/03/1917	14/03/1917
War Diary	R.5.c.33. R.5.d.87. 5.31.b.0.0. G.31.b.96. R.5.d.68. R.5.b.37. R.5.c.4.8. R.5.a.55. R.5.a.55. L.15.c.8. W.11.c.30.	14/03/1917	14/03/1917
War Diary	R.33.b.55. Nab.junc R.11.c.5.3. R.5.a.46.	15/03/1917	15/03/1917
War Diary	L.35.c.45. G.31.b.0.0.	15/03/1917	15/03/1917
War Diary	G.31.b.0.0. G.26.c.4.2. G.27.a.	15/03/1917	15/03/1917
War Diary	R.5.c.33. R.5.d.87. K.11.c.3.0. R.5.a.72.	15/03/1917	15/03/1917
War Diary	R.5.c.48. R.5.a.55. R.5.d.0.8. R.5.d.7.M.Z.c.7.1. M.Z.d.35.	15/03/1917	15/03/1917
War Diary	R.22.d.41. R.11.c.53. R.5.a.46. R.5.c.33. R.5.d.87. R.5.a.48. R.5.a.55.	16/03/1917	16/03/1917
War Diary	Miraumont-Pys	16/03/1917	16/03/1917
War Diary	Pys-Cemetry.	16/03/1917	16/03/1917
War Diary	R.5.c.55. R.5.a.7.2. W.11.c.30.	16/03/1917	16/03/1917
War Diary	R.5.c.33. R.6.a.35. R.22.d.451. R.11.c.53.	17/03/1917	17/03/1917
War Diary	Miraumont Pys	17/03/1917	17/03/1917
War Diary	Peiit Miraumont.	17/03/1917	17/03/1917
War Diary	R.10.a.43. W.11.c.30.	17/03/1917	17/03/1917
War Diary	Miraumont Irles R.5.a.	18/03/1917	18/03/1917
War Diary	Miraumont Irles W.11.c.30.	18/03/1917	18/03/1917
War Diary	Achiet Le Grand.	18/03/1917	18/03/1917
War Diary	Miraumont Pys	19/03/1917	19/03/1917
War Diary	Peiit Miraumont R.5.c.33-Irles	19/03/1917	19/03/1917
War Diary	Achiet Le Grand W.11.c.3.0.	19/03/1917	23/03/1917
War Diary	Saleux.	24/03/1917	25/03/1917
War Diary	Steenbecque Sta.	26/03/1917	26/03/1917
War Diary	Boeseghem.	27/03/1917	31/03/1917
War Diary		01/03/1917	31/03/1917
War Diary	Boeseghem.	01/04/1917	20/04/1917
War Diary	Lambres.	21/04/1917	21/04/1917
War Diary	Bethune.	22/04/1917	23/04/1917
War Diary	Petit Servins.	24/04/1917	24/04/1917
War Diary	Aux Rietz.	25/04/1917	30/04/1917
War Diary	Boisengham.	01/04/1917	14/04/1917
War Diary	Bethune.	23/04/1917	23/04/1917
War Diary	Aure Raity.	26/04/1917	26/04/1917
War Diary	Beaurains.	30/04/1917	31/05/1917
War Diary		02/05/1917	21/05/1917
War Diary		20/05/1917	31/05/1917
War Diary	Sector Facing S.W. of Cherisy.	01/06/1917	17/06/1917
War Diary	Coigneux.	18/06/1917	22/06/1917
War Diary	Hoogegraaf Cab.	23/06/1917	30/06/1917
War Diary		01/06/1917	29/06/1917
War Diary	Busse Boom.	01/07/1917	06/07/1917
War Diary	Zillebeke Bund.	07/07/1917	23/07/1917
War Diary	Dickebusch	24/07/1917	31/07/1917
War Diary	Dickebusch	10/07/1917	03/08/1917
War Diary	Zillebeke Bund.	04/08/1917	11/08/1917
War Diary	Dickebush	12/08/1917	13/08/1917
War Diary	Abeele	14/08/1917	15/08/1917
War Diary	Sprenn-Kot	16/08/1917	17/08/1917
War Diary	Millain.	18/08/1917	31/08/1917

War Diary		01/08/1917	13/08/1917
War Diary		12/08/1917	12/08/1917
War Diary		09/08/1917	22/08/1917
War Diary	Millam	01/09/1917	15/09/1917
War Diary	Sprenwkot	16/09/1917	28/09/1917
War Diary	Brielen.	29/09/1917	30/09/1917
War Diary		04/09/1917	11/09/1917
War Diary		09/09/1917	29/09/1917
War Diary	Brielen B.30.a.7.7. Sheet 28. N.W.	01/10/1917	15/11/1917
War Diary		19/10/1917	28/10/1917
War Diary	C.13.a.2.3. Reference Bixsehoote.	01/11/1917	04/11/1917
War Diary	Hampton Camp.	05/11/1917	30/11/1917
War Diary		05/11/1917	05/11/1917
War Diary		04/11/1917	26/11/1917
War Diary		22/11/1917	22/11/1917
War Diary	Ref. Bixshoote and Boesinghe 1/10,000	01/12/1917	16/12/1917
War Diary	N of Proven (Hazebrouck 5.a.).	17/12/1917	27/12/1917
War Diary	Sheet 29. W.25.c.b.5.	28/12/1917	31/12/1917
War Diary		02/12/1917	28/12/1917
War Diary		26/12/1917	26/12/1917
War Diary	Sheet 19. W.25.b.6.5.	01/01/1918	01/01/1918
War Diary	Hampton Camp Sheet 28. B.11.a.2.3.	02/01/1918	30/01/1918
War Diary	Sheet 28.A.9.c.5.4.	31/01/1918	31/01/1918
War Diary		03/01/1918	28/01/1918
War Diary	Sheet 27. D.11.c.3.7.	01/02/1918	01/02/1918
War Diary	Sheet 27. D.8.c.7.7.	02/02/1918	08/02/1918
War Diary	Sheet St Quemtion 18 Varesnes.	09/02/1918	11/02/1918
War Diary	Sheet 70.D. A.4.d.3.6.	12/02/1918	25/02/1918
War Diary	Sheet 66.C.M.36.d.7.9.	26/02/1918	28/02/1918
War Diary		02/02/1918	28/02/1918
Heading	18th Div. War Diary 92nd Field Company, R.E. March 1918.		
War Diary	Sheet 66.c. S.W. M.36.d.6.8.	01/03/1918	20/03/1918
War Diary	Ref. St Zuentin Sheet.	21/03/1918	31/03/1918
War Diary		04/03/1918	29/03/1918
Heading	18th Div. 92nd Field Company, R.E. April 1918.		
War Diary	Boves Sheet 62.D. T.16.a.9.5.	01/04/1918	02/04/1918
War Diary	O.36.C.3.4.	03/04/1918	04/04/1918
War Diary	Boves.	05/04/1918	11/04/1918
War Diary	Amiens.	12/04/1918	30/04/1918
War Diary		01/04/1918	23/04/1918
War Diary	C.5.a.6.3. Sheet 62.D.	01/05/1918	31/05/1918
War Diary		02/05/1918	02/05/1918
War Diary		01/05/1918	19/05/1918
War Diary		18/05/1918	28/05/1918
War Diary	C.5.C.8.7. Sheet 62.D.	01/06/1918	30/06/1918
War Diary		04/06/1918	18/06/1918
War Diary		16/06/1918	22/06/1918
War Diary	C.5.C.5.5. Senlis Pheicad Sheet.	01/07/1918	12/07/1918
War Diary	Amins Map 17.	13/07/1918	29/07/1918
War Diary	Sheet 62 D	30/07/1918	31/07/1918
War Diary		06/07/1918	06/07/1918
War Diary		05/07/1918	16/07/1918
War Diary		15/07/1918	28/07/1918
Heading	18th Division Engineers 92nd Field Company, R.E. August. 1918.		

Type	Description	From	To
Miscellaneous	C.R.E. 18th Division.	01/11/1918	01/11/1918
War Diary	Sheet 62 D.I.5.d.9.8.	01/08/1918	09/08/1918
War Diary	Senlis Special Sheet V.27.b.5.1.	10/08/1918	21/08/1918
War Diary	Becourt Sheet.	22/08/1918	24/08/1918
War Diary	V.27.b.5.1.	25/08/1918	25/08/1918
War Diary	Becourt Sheet.	26/08/1918	29/08/1918
War Diary	Albert Combined Sheet.	30/08/1918	31/08/1918
War Diary		01/08/1918	26/08/1918
War Diary	D.24.a.4.2. Sheet 62.C.	21/09/1918	24/09/1918
War Diary	D.4.C.3.9.	25/09/1918	30/09/1918
War Diary		06/09/1918	25/09/1918
War Diary	Albert Combined S.29.b.8.3.	01/09/1918	02/09/1918
War Diary	B.4.a.2.9.	02/09/1918	04/09/1918
War Diary	S.28.b.4.4.	05/09/1918	15/09/1918
War Diary	Sheet 62.b. N.E. D.24.a.4.2.	16/09/1918	20/09/1918
Miscellaneous	C.R.E. 18th Division.	01/11/1918	01/11/1918
War Diary	Nurlu D.4.C.3.9. Sheet 62.b.	01/10/1918	02/10/1918
War Diary	Contay.	03/10/1918	19/10/1918
War Diary	Elincourt (S.I. Zuentin Sheet).	20/10/1918	23/10/1918
War Diary	LE Cateav K.35.d.3.1. Sheet 51.B. N.E.	24/10/1918	30/10/1918
War Diary	K.34.C.5.4.	31/10/1918	31/10/1918
War Diary		05/10/1918	25/10/1918
War Diary		21/10/1918	21/10/1918
War Diary	K.34.C.5.4. Sheet 57.B.N.E.	01/11/1918	04/11/1918
War Diary	F.28.C.7.4. Sheet 57.B.N.E.	05/11/1918	07/11/1918
War Diary	C.8.C.9.4. Sheet 57.A.N.W.	08/11/1918	09/11/1918
War Diary	C.10.C.4.6.	10/11/1918	17/11/1918
War Diary	Maurois Sheet 57.B. U.a.9.6.	19/11/1918	30/11/1918
War Diary		02/11/1918	29/11/1918
War Diary	Elincourt Sheet 57 B U.3.a.9.6.	01/12/1918	16/12/1918
War Diary	Villers Outreaux Sheet 57 B T.15. Central.	17/12/1918	31/12/1918
War Diary		07/12/1918	30/12/1918
War Diary	Sheet 57.B. T.15.d.1.9.	01/01/1919	18/01/1919
War Diary	J.22. Central,	19/01/1919	31/01/1919
War Diary		02/01/1919	31/01/1919
War Diary	Sheet 57.B J.22. Central.	01/02/1919	15/02/1919
War Diary	I.30.a.7.2.	16/02/1919	28/02/1919
War Diary	18th Div.	01/02/1919	26/02/1919
War Diary		20/02/1919	27/02/1919
War Diary	I.30.a.7.2.	01/03/1919	31/03/1919
War Diary		04/03/1919	26/03/1919
War Diary	Sheet 57.b.I.30.a.7.2.	01/04/1919	30/04/1919
War Diary		01/04/1919	28/04/1919
Miscellaneous	O i/c 3rd Echelon Details Balfour House Finsbury Pavement London E.C.	02/07/1919	02/07/1919
War Diary	Sheet 57.B. I.23.a.7.2.	01/06/1919	30/06/1919
War Diary		06/06/1919	08/06/1919
War Diary		01/06/1919	01/06/1919
War Diary	Sheet 57.B. I.30.a.7.2.	14/06/1919	03/08/1919

WO 95/2027/3

10TH DIVISION

92ND FIELD COY. R.E.

SEPT 1915 – AUG 1919

D/7517

18th Kurrain.

92 w/ 7.C.R.E.
Vol I

July & Aug 15.

Confidential.

War Diary
of
92 Field Co. R.E.
from 27.7.15 to 31.8.15.

Army Form C. 2118.

WAR DIARY
or
INTELLIGENCE SUMMARY.
(Erase heading not required.)

92 Field Co. R.E.   Sheet No. 1.

Instructions regarding War Diaries and Intelligence Summaries are contained in F.S. Regs., Part II. and the Staff Manual respectively. Title pages will be prepared in manuscript.

Place	Date	Hour	Summary of Events and Information	Remarks and references to Appendices
SOUTHAMPTON	27.7.15		92 Field Co. R.E. embarked.	N.L.
HAVRE	28.7.15		Disembarked at HAVRE and went into rest camp.	N.L.
HAVRE	29.7.15		Entrained at 2.0 p.m. detrained at LONGUEAU 3 miles S.E. of AMIENS at 4 p.m. marched to billets at COISY (Map AMIENS 1/2)	N.L.
COISY	30.7.15 31.7.11 1.8.11 2.8.11 3.8.11		In billets: improving water supplies. and practice in pontooning. practice in bomb throwing.	N.L. N.L.
			On 3rd Co. inspected woods at MONTONVILLERS & FLESSELS & BERTANGLES with view of cutting timber for work work. Suitable woods at all these places.	N.L.
	4.8.11		Coy to SENLIS & MILLENCOURT in billets	N.L.
	5.8.15		92 Co marched to MILLENCOURT. C.S. X" Corps pointed out approx line of trenches to be constructed and allotted portion to 92 & 80 F. Co.	N.L.
MILLENCOURT	6.8.15.		Saw Mayors of neighbouring communes re cutting corn.	N.L.
	7.8.15		Met Mayor of BOUZINCOURT re ground and printed out fields to be cut. wheat type barley not rye.	N.L.
	8.8.11		C.S. X" Corps inspected proposed line laid out	N.L.
	9.8.15		Laying out trenches. Received orders from C.S. X" Corps as to alterations to same. Visited SENLIS to see Major Robinson re alterations.	N.L.

1577 Wt. W10791/1773 500,000 1/15 D.D.&L. A.D.S.S./Forms/C. 2118.

Army Form C. 2118
Sheet 2.

WAR DIARY
or
INTELLIGENCE SUMMARY

(Erase heading not required.)

92 Field Co. R.E.

Instructions regarding War Diaries and Intelligence Summaries are contained in F.S. Regs., Part II. and the Staff Manual respectively. Title Pages will be prepared in manuscript.

Place	Date	Hour	Summary of Events and Information	Remarks and references to Appendices
MILLENCOURT	10.9.15	—	Laid out line of trenches round village and new village. 400 men of 6th Entrenching Battalion commenced work.	
"	11.9.15		6th Entrenching Bn. Entrenching round village. Works inspected by G.O.C. & C.E. XI Corps	
"	12.9.15		6th Ent. Bn. working on trenches. Works visited by C.R.E. 18th Division.	
"	13.9.15		} Supervision of 6th Ent. Bn. on trenches.	N.S.L.
"	14.9.15			
"	15.9.15			
"	16.9.15			
"	17.9.15		do. do. Works inspected in detail by C.E. XI Corps in morning. Major Lewis Capt Wright.	
"	18.9.15		Reconnaissance for tank Jails of MILLENCOURT in a.m. Reconnaissance for extension made. Work continued on trenches.	N.S.L.
"	19.9.15		do. do. C.E. X Corps. &c inspected proposed site of works	N.S.L.
"	20.9.15		do. do. extension of trenches Took over extension of trenches being made by 80th Field Co. in front of SENLIS.	N.S.L.
"	21.9.15		Work continued on trenches. Laid out positions for extension of works north of MILLENCOURT.	N.S.L.
"	22.9.15		Rest day. Inspected SENLIS Trenches with C.E. XI Corps.	N.S.L.

Army Form C. 2118

Sheet N° 3.

WAR DIARY
or
INTELLIGENCE SUMMARY

92. Field Co. R.E.

(Erase heading not required.)

Instructions regarding War Diaries and Intelligence Summaries are contained in F.S. Regs., Part II. and the Staff Manual respectively. Title Pages will be prepared in manuscript.

Place	Date	Hour	Summary of Events and Information	Remarks and references to Appendices
MILLENCOURT	23.8.15		Work on 2nd Line Trenches continued.	N.S.L.
	24.8.15		do. do.	N.S.L.
	25.8.15		do. do.	N.S.L.
	26.8.15		Work on 2nd Line Trenches continued	N.S.L.
	27.8.15		do. do.	N.S.L.
	28.8.15		do. do. Trenches of SENLIS and north of SENLIS handed over to 143 Trenches Co. D.S.	N.S.L.
	29.8.15		Work on 1st Line Trenches continued.	N.S.L.
	30.8.15		do. do. do.	N.S.L.
	31.8.15		do. do. do.	N.S.L.
			Generally speaking the from 6.8.15 - 16 - 31.8.15; The company has been employed in selecting sites for redoubts: laying them out and revetting infantry trenches: parties of about 2000 - 3000 men. and along the technical work of revetting and tunnelling, and building bomb proof dug outs with 10 feet overhead cover. Casting expanded concrete slabs for roofs of dug outs.	N.S.L.

12/7517

18th Division

92nd F.C. R.E.
Vol 2

Sep 1/15

Aug '19

Confidential

War Diary

of

92nd Field Co. R.E.

from 1-9-15 to 30-9-15

WAR DIARY
INTELLIGENCE SUMMARY

Army Form C. 2118

Place	Date	Hour	Summary of Events and Information	Remarks and references to Appendices
MILLENCOURT.	1.9.15 to 20.9.15	—	92: Field Co. R.E. Working under orders of X.th Corps. The company continued work on the 2.Line (X.th Corps Line) of Barricle Defences on the road of this Entrenching Battalion and carrying out the more technical work of erecting fire steps and revetting dug outs, and making reinforced slabs for the roofs of dug outs. Details of work. (a) Defence of village of MILLENCOURT by construction of Trenches and dug outs round the village and construction of wire entanglement. (b) Construction of four steel adrods (bid for 2 Co. bid for 1 Co. Each) with dug outs and wire entanglement. (c) Reconstruction of old French Line East of village of MILLENCOURT. N.B. dug outs constructed with floor level 14 feet below	182

WAR DIARY or INTELLIGENCE SUMMARY

Army Form C. 2118
Sheet 2.

Place	Date	Hour	Summary of Events and Information	Remarks and references to Appendices
MILLENCOURT	19.9.15 to 20.9.15	—	92' Field Coy R.E. Ground line – 6 feet head room. and two feet above ground line. Some dug out roofed with timber others with iron girders and reinforced concrete slabs.	h.S.L
DEARNANCOURT	20.9.15 to 30.9.15	—	Company marched to DEARNANCOURT (less 1 section viz N°2 section) and rejoined the 18th Division. N°2 section was left at MILLENCOURT to supervise work on Corps line. The company was allotted to the 53rd Infantry Brigade to work on the trenches in D3 & E, sectors and employed in improving the trenches and communication trenches. New support trenches laid out by Capt King 80 t. Field Co R.E. & Lt Tyler 92' Field Co R.E. behind firing line in D, E, where were dug by the 8/Suss x Pioneers & R.W.Wd Regt and R.S. on the two following nights by J.Tyler. Support trenches laid out at night and dug by Sussex Pioneers in D3. French ladders made for an attack and material collected for an advance. Sailly Road over trenches bridged in five places to carry artillery in case of an advance.	h.S.L

WAR DIARY
or
INTELLIGENCE SUMMARY

Sheet 3.

92nd Field Co. R.E.

Casualties during month of September 1915:

Officers NIL.

Week ending 3.9.15: 1. 2nd Capt. (sick). 2 Sappers (sick). (Casuals). 1 Sapper
      "   10.9.15: 1 Sapper 1 Driver joined.
      "   17.9.15: 1 Sapper (bomb) accidental. 1 Driver sick
      "   24.9.15: 1 Sapper joined
      "   30.9.15: 1 Capt.(sick) 1 Driver (sick).
                       3 Sappers joined 1 driver joined

                       NIL.

                                 N.E. Leermyrn lt.
                                 O.C. 92nd Field Coy R.E.

N.E.L.

12/
7517

18th Kwanun

92nd F.C. R.E.
Rot: #3
Oct 15

Confidential

War Diary
of
92nd Field Co. R.E.
from 1-10-15 to 31-10-15

Army Form C. 2118

WAR DIARY
or
INTELLIGENCE SUMMARY
(Erase heading not required.)

Place	Date	Hour	Summary of Events and Information	Remarks and references to Appendices
DERNANCOURT	1.10.15 to 31.10.15	—	**92 Field Co. R.E.** The Company during the month has been employed as follows. Billeted in DERNANCOURT with exception of No. 2. Section noted below — No. 4 Section working in sector D3 with the infantry 8/ East Surrey R and 7 West Surrey (The Queens) making dug outs, roofing dug outs in support line, opening up dug out bloom in — starting machinery in boden mineral shaft and in ALBERT and making Hewlett Pans — laying BOARD WALK in communication trenches. No. 2 Section working under C.E. X I. Corps at MILLENCOURT on 2nd Line (Corps Line) of redoubts and trenches till the 15th on which date it joined the Company and worked in BECOURT WOOD (E.1) in the construction of BECOURT Redoubt, assisting infantry working parties of 100 men supplied daily from the 55th Infantry Brigade. Work carried out consisting parapet of old FRENCH line and construction of 8 dug outs — No. 3 Section work on Intermediate Line making two redoubts with west of BECORDEL assisting infantry working parties supplied by 54 & 53 Infantry Brigades. Redoubts for one company and one platoon each.	

Army Form C. 2118

2 Sheet

WAR DIARY
or
INTELLIGENCE SUMMARY

(Erase heading not required.)

Instructions regarding War Diaries and Intelligence Summaries are contained in F.S. Regs., Part II. and the Staff Manual respectively. Title Pages will be prepared in manuscript.

Place	Date	Hour	Summary of Events and Information	Remarks and references to Appendices
DERNANCOURT.	1.10.16 to 31.10.16		92: Field Co:R.E.	

No 4 Section assisting infantry in E. Section 7 East Kent R. (The Buffs) & 7 R.W. Kent R. — laying board walk in communication trenches — making bomb stores in support line — repairing damaged dug out and making new dug out made by the infantry — making traverses in communication trenches. —

Head Quarters of Co. arranging for materials for sections — opening locks in Head quarters of Co. —

DERNANCOURT.— improving billets — erection of circular saw bench — working rules — talks — training infantry detachments in the erection of barbed wire entanglements by night. Section of water troughs and making watering place for 55th Dy Brigade

Men used in detachment to work under CRE 18th Division in workshops. and making drying rooms and bathing Establishment.

1875 Wt. W593/826 1,000,000 4/15 J.B.C. & A. A.D.S.S./Forms/C. 2118.

Army Form C. 2118

WAR DIARY
or
INTELLIGENCE SUMMARY

(Erase heading not required.)

3" Sheet.

Instructions regarding War Diaries and Intelligence Summaries are contained in F.S. Regs., Part II. and the Staff Manual respectively. Title Pages will be prepared in manuscript.

Place	Date	Hour	Summary of Events and Information	Remarks and references to Appendices
DERNANCOURT.	1.10.16 to 31.10.16		Accompanied ~~Reconnaissance Wednesday~~ C.R.E. 15th. to select site of redoubt in intermediate line 92 Field Co R.E. Reconnaissance made of BECOURT WOOD to select school and site for redoubt to E, Leclo.	
	19th		C.E. X" Corps inspected D3 or E, Leclo.	
	31st		O.C. C.R.S. to make reconnaissance of TAMBOUR in D3 & find new dumping ground for excavation from mine. Site selected and arrangements made to commence work on the following night.	
			Casualties during month.	
			WEEK ending.	
	8.10.16:		nil.	
	15.10.16:		2 Sappers (Sick). O.R.11 Corpl. joined	
	22.10.16:		2 Sappers. 1 Driver. (Accidently through bayonet being WOUNDED unexploded. Shell. Court of enquiry found that 1 Sapper + 1 Driver were negligent. 2 Sappers 1 Driver joined.	
	29.10.16:		1 Section 107th Field Co R.E. joined for work on 28th Sheet.	
			Left on the 31st.	
				H.S. Lee Marshe O.G. F Coy. R.E.

2nd F.C. R.E.
Vol 4

121/76214

18th K Wraun

Nov 15

92nd Field Coy R.E.

Diary

from 1-11-15 to 30-11-15

Army Form C. 2118

WAR DIARY or INTELLIGENCE SUMMARY
(Erase heading not required.)

92. Field Co. R.E.

Place	Date	Hour	Summary of Events and Information	Remarks and references to Appendices
DEAN AN COURT	1.11.15 to 6.11.15		1.11.15: Construction of 5" dug out in STONEHAVEN Street E, Sector handed over to 8/ Royal Sussex Pioneers owing to amount of work in the hands of the company. 2.11.15: Site selected with O.C. R.W. Kent Regt. for 4 dug out to be made in BON ACCORD Street and handed over to Sussex Pioneers. No 1 Section commenced: (a) commenced work by night making new dumping ground by building sand bag breastwork for excavation from TAMBOUR MINES. (b) making field aspen in ALBERT. (c) made sample revêtment in TAMBOUR as sand bags told not stand owing to ground having been very torn by enemy's mines.	Ash
			Timber frames made from scrum timber. The slips made by plank slip where required.	
			(c) continued laying board walk. Is sawn poplar boards 2" thick on cross sleepers. Width of walk 1'-6" made from 2 or 3 boards. This is better and quicker to make than grid or gratings but is very slippery in wet weather.	
			(d) Reconnaissance for laying in water to BECOURT CHATEAU.	
			(9) Roofing dug out in SURREY Street.	

Army Form C. 2118

WAR DIARY
or
INTELLIGENCE SUMMARY
(Erase heading not required.)

92 Field Coy.

Place	Date	Hour	Summary of Events and Information	Remarks and references to Appendices
DERNANCOURT.	1.11.15 to 6.11.15.		No 2 Section worked with 8/ East Surrey Regt. as working party on BECOURT WOOD. Also making 8 dugouts and commenced roofing 6. Making up trench fire parapet and fire step. and hurdles in the EMBANKMENT & BON ACCORD STREET. Sect. found work in ABERDEEN AVENUE. On 6.11.15 No 2 Section marched back to DERNANCOURT and went into billets. No 3 Section with working parties from 54th and 63rd Infantry Brigade. Continued construction of redoubts rook west of BECOURT on intermediate line. On 2.11.15 commenced laying one mile of trench tramway ALBERT BECOURT commenced track. No 3 & No 4 Section working in DERNANCOURT on works employed. and working Creaton sawn. Market Forge. 88th Inf. Brigade Carpenters workshops at DERNANCOURT.	252
	7.11.15 to 13.11.15.		Head Quarters and No 2 Section continued work on works employed in DERNANCOURT and started Brigade Workshops. Ten men from 253 Tunneling Co. attached to 92 Field Co. R.E. for road repairs in the village. (Creaton saw bench running two shifts daily. No 1 Section. completed making iron work for 18 Allenhut frames in ALBERT. continued working front face of TAMBOUR 27 yards up to date completed	

1875 Wt. W593/826 1,000,000 4/15 J.B.C. & A. A.D.S.S./Forms/C. 2118.

WAR DIARY or INTELLIGENCE SUMMARY

(Erase heading not required.)

Army Form C. 2118

G.2 Field Coy.

Place	Date	Hour	Summary of Events and Information	Remarks and references to Appendices
DERNAN-COURT	14.11.15 to 20.11.15		from E. Corkers to BECOURT CHATEAU. (400 yards) Moved 1600 gallon tank from front of Chateau to back and plugged bullet holes –	
			N° 4 Section. Commenced mining assisted by infantry 4 dug outs 24' long and 15 feet deep. In SHUTTLE LANE. E. Laying board walk ABERDEEN AVENUE E. Taking rept.	
			Off. large dug out in BECOURT CHATEAU assisted by infantry.	h.S.L.
	21.11.15 to h.S.L. 30 & 27.11.15		N° 2 Section relieved N° 4 Section. N° 2 gang m6 dug out in BECOURT & and N° 4 Billets in DERNANCOURT –	
			All work continued as last week.	
			N° Section preparing timber for roof of dug out in TANGIER – D3.	
			Major Lees proceeded to HEILLY and acted as C.R.E. from 17.11.15 to 25.11.15. Capt Wright proceeded on leave 26.11.15.	h.S.L.

Army Form C. 2118

WAR DIARY
or
INTELLIGENCE SUMMARY
(Erase heading not required.)

92 Field Co R.E.

Instructions regarding War Diaries and Intelligence Summaries are contained in F. S. Regs., Part II. and the Staff Manual respectively. Title Pages will be prepared in manuscript.

Place	Date	Hour	Summary of Events and Information	Remarks and references to Appendices
DERNANCOURT	7.11.15 to 13.11.15		No 1 Section (front) Assisting infantry revetting front faces of Tambour. Laying bound walk for mines truck to remove sandbags to new dumping ground. Anging 5' dug out in D3.	
			No 3 Section. Continued work on BECORDEL REDOUBTS and cutting timber for roofs of dug outs. Commenced gun emplacement north of BECORDEL (working at night) — continued laying gratings in BECOURT- ALBERT communication trench.	
			No 4 Section. Continued work on BECOURT REDUIT. Continued laying bound walk in ABERDEEN AVENUE- shifting BOMB STORES in E1.	h.s.
do. do.	14.11.15 to 20.11.15		H.Q'rs and No 2 Section. as continued with as from 7.11.15 to 13.11.15.	
			No 1 Section. Continued revetting front face of TAMBOUR. not occupied nor shell- completed bound walk from 16 new stumps to sandbag and laid guide rails for trollies. 200 yard 24' dug out in D3 sector.	
			No 3 Section. Continued work as from 7.11.15 to 13.11.15. and in addition extended 1" water pipe to D3 lookout. 100 yards. and laid 1½" water pipe	h.s.

1875 Wt. W593/826 1,000,000 4/15 J.B.C. & A. A.D.S.S./Forms/C. 2118.

Army Form C.2118

WAR DIARY
or
INTELLIGENCE SUMMARY
(Erase heading not required.)

Instructions regarding War Diaries and Intelligence Summaries are contained in F.S. Regs., Part II. and the Staff Manual respectively. Title Pages will be prepared in manuscript.

Place	Date	Hour	Summary of Events and Information	Remarks and references to Appendices
DEARHACOURT.	1.11.15 to 30.11.15		Return of Casualties during month of November.	
			Week ending	
			5.11.15 — Nil.	
			12.11.15 — 2 Sappers 1 Driver joined (28 reinforcements).	
			10 Sappers from 253 Tunnelling Co attached to 7th Coca Work -	
			19.11.16 — 1 Capt. joined (reinforcement).	
			26.11.15 — 1 Sapper joined (reinforcement).	
			S.M. Wadeson evacuated sick to Base on 13.11.15 has not joined again.	

N.S. Lee Major.
OC 172 Field Coy RE.
30.11.15

92ⁿᵈ F.e.R.E.
Pot: 5

121/7910

18th Feb

Confidential

War Diary of
92nd Field Co RE
from 1-12-15
to 31-12-15

Army Form C. 2118

92nd Field Co R.E.

December 1915. Sheet 1

WAR DIARY
or
INTELLIGENCE SUMMARY
(Erase heading not required.)

Instructions regarding War Diaries and Intelligence Summaries are contained in F.S. Regs, Part II. and the Staff Manual respectively. Title Pages will be prepared in manuscript.

Place	Date	Hour	Summary of Events and Information	Remarks and references to Appendices
DERNAN- COURT.	1.12.15 to 5.12.15		Head Quarters and No. 4 Section continued working in DERNANCOURT. Executes new Bench. Carpenters Shop. improvements to billets. Spanning road DERNANCOURT.	
			No.1 Section continued working in TAMBOUR. 38 yards in the west making total of 169 yards. Noted small dug out in D3 Sector (Sunny Street) 10' × 9'.	
			No.2 Section continued mining from dug outs in E1 Sector Shrublle Lane.	
			" laying board walk in Aberdeen Avenue E1.	
			No.3 Section " work on Stonework. One redoubt north of BECORDEL.	
			" Repaired laying of French gratings in BECOURT-ALBERT Communication trench.	
			Cut road metal by night from ALBERT-FRICOURT road to road upkeep - Continued making gun position for A.T.C. north of BECORDEL at night - & getting pneumatic pumps into position and tuition for pumping water from well in BECOURT Chateau.	
			Leaving the pud road. This days heavy frost have been followed by heavy rain - The frost disintegrated the chalk and the trenches have fallen in.	

Army Form C. 2118

WAR DIARY
INTELLIGENCE SUMMARY
(Erase heading not required.)

92 Field Co. R.E. Sheet 2

Place	Date	Hour	Summary of Events and Information	Remarks and references to Appendices
DERNANCOURT	1.12.15 to 3.12.15	—	The experience of the last week shews the absolute necessity of adhering to the rules and principles laid down in Military Engineering for construction of trenches, especially under the following heads:— Sides of trenches must have a batter. They are invariably dug too vertical — berms should be left — drainage should be provided by cutting short lengths of trench at an angle to fire or communication trenches. There are much better than sump pits. Trenches should be graded during construction and not left till opportunity as this means that trenches are not graded. Trench gradings should be provided as soon as trenches are constructed. Board walks are better than trench gradings. Any fallen earth can easily be scraped off and the scrapings gradient is obtained. Sandbag revetments should be constructed so that each course is in section at right angles to the slope — and the ground cut away to make this to be done. It might be a help if the diagrams in the Notes from the Front shewed a batter to sides of trenches instead of straight sides —	

WAR DIARY
or
INTELLIGENCE SUMMARY

Army Form C. 2118
Sheet 3

Place	Date	Hour	Summary of Events and Information	Remarks and references to Appendices
BERTHEN COURT	6.12.15 to 20.12.15		Wire Obstacles in No 2 Section reinforced in older Construction - making second & existing Section of information Mark 8'4"x 3'0" Inspection sliding hoarded in making of the deep moat 1931 -. Making W.C. Frames any size from 3 ratings have been made instead of board walk on this take guide "b by 3'" that three sheets is in front has small Mills - Second walk No.1 Section Continued making file staffs and erecting TAMBOUR D3. Topping up dugouts in 33 1/2. Completed 2" M.T. storing first used your Improvement in D3 trenches Inspectors from gun trenches D3. No.2 Section Continued work on intermediate line DECOUDER. Their passerelle revenues and Shyne "A" pumped out shell "WELSH" "SUTTERR" "OXFORD" has two deep with 12 feet of water. Pump not sufficiently powerful to take blocked drain supply to D1 sewer found obstructed Image tanks. 5th Section mounted out to BECOURT CHATEAU on 6th and relieved No 2 section and continued making two dug outs 24 feet long 7 feet wide 15 feet deep in SHUTTLE LANE E1. Sappers working Mine Shafts Infantry carrying & removing material tiring framing in large deep out in BECOURT CHATEAU E1.	WSL

Army Form C. 2118

WAR DIARY or INTELLIGENCE SUMMARY

92nd Field Coy. R.E. Sheet 4

(Erase heading not required.)

Place	Date	Hour	Summary of Events and Information	Remarks and references to Appendices
DERNANCOURT	21.12.15 to 27.12.15		Head Qrs and No. 4 Section continued work as last week. Cies supplied men for fixing wiring machines and Horsfall detector. Commenced resinking roads in DERNANCOURT.	
			No. 1 Section working in TAMBOUR. D3 making new fire parapet to take place of portion about 30' long blown in by enemy's mine. The wiring showed that westward of TAMBOUR wire wood frames and iron sheeting saved a large portion of his face from being blown in.	
			No. 2 Section in BECOURT CHATEAU completed 2 dug outs in SHUTTLE LANE continued work on two other dug outs SHUTTLE LANE and dug out BECOURT CHATEAU.	
			No. 3 Section continued work on intermediate line.	
do do	28.12.15 to 31.12.15		Work continued as above. No. 1 Section built up temporary shelters to strengthen westward of TAMBOUR. To take most of our mine. No damage done by mine. Buried to repair damage from hostile bombardment. Working wires attempted by effects of lachrymatory shell.	
	28.12.15		No. 3 Section to attached to TAEUX to work under C.R.E. in improving and augmenting accommodation. Four men of No. 4 Section took new work in intermediate line.	

N.S. Lee Meyer
O.C. 92 Field Coy

Army Form C. 2118

92' Field Coy. Sheet 5"

WAR DIARY
or
INTELLIGENCE SUMMARY
(Erase heading not required.)

Place	Date	Hour	Summary of Events and Information	Remarks and references to Appendices

Casualties for Month of December.

Week ending 3.12.15: NIL.

10.12.15: The Sapper. No 51330 Sapper McMeion killed by accidental discharge of rifle in billet when being cleaned by another man —

17.12.15. 2" Lieut ROWE E.S. joined company 14.12.15.

24.12.15: The Sapper sent home to England for munition work —

31.12.15: The Driver joined as reinforcement.

H.S. Lewpoint.
Lt. 92 Field Co RE.

92nd F.C.R.E.
Vol: 6

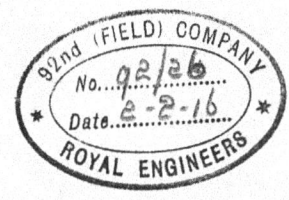

Confidential

War Diary of

92nd Field Co R.E.

From 1-1-16 To 31-1-16

R.G. Wright
Capt R.E.
for COMdg 92nd (Fd.) Co. R.E.

WAR DIARY or INTELLIGENCE SUMMARY

Army Form C. 2118

92: Field Co. R.E. Sheet 1

Place	Date	Hour	Summary of Events and Information	Remarks and references to Appendices
DE RANANCOURT.	1.1.16 to 8.1.16.		Head Quarters and N°4 Section. Running circular saw 14 hours daily - making hooks & clamps and cutting shelving. and work generally in shops - filling timber to saw bench. Six men working on Intermediate Line at BECORDEL. completing dug out and wire entanglement. N°3 Section working under C.A.S. 18th Division at TAEUX improving billets and providing married accommodation - N°1 Section working on D3. repairing TAMBOUR hornline. cutting timber to dug out - Commenced repairing three dug outs in SHAREY Street. Repaired roof of dug out in TANGIER. N°2 Section up in BECOURT CHATEAU - extended water supply to D3 wash house. filled and ran pulsometer pumps to try and clear well Chateau well - but pump not sufficiently powerful to deal with intake of water in well - Work continued on BECOURT CHATEAU dug out - Sites selected for 3 cut & cover dug outs in SHUTTLE LANE and sites marked out by L⁺ Nunn on 5.1.16. N°13 Platoon D.C. Sussex & Pioneers. commenced work on E. deep water on 7.1.16 working under O.C. 92 Field Co. R.E.	hsd

Army Form C. 2118.

WAR DIARY
or
INTELLIGENCE SUMMARY.

98th Field Co R.E. Sheet 2

(Erase heading not required.)

Instructions regarding War Diaries and Intelligence Summaries are contained in F. S. Regs., Part II. and the Staff Manual respectively. Title pages will be prepared in manuscript.

Place	Date	Hour	Summary of Events and Information	Remarks and references to Appendices
DERAT DERNANCOURT	9.1.16 to 15.1.16		H.Q and No 4 Section. Running circular saw over 14 hr daily - making trench gratings and cutting sheeting for dug outs etc. Work generally in shops - e.g. hand-braces lined with tin, rifle-grenade buttress etc. 1 N.C.O. and 4 men working on intermediate line North of BECORDEL. No 1 Section working in D3. entai-propping dugouts - repairs in TAMBOUR DU CLOS. Bourreyeu steel shelter segments up to SHUTTLE LANE. - drilling angle iron for steel shelters in workshop in ALBERT. This Section relieved No 3 on 14.1.16. No 4 Section working in E1. Shelter dugout - completed gratings from CHATEAU down HUNTLEY ST. - entai-propping dugouts in SHUTTLE LANE. Dismantled Petroenein will at BECOURT. Water laid on to D3 work house. Extra 200 gallon tank fixed. No 3 Section. Working under C.R.E. at TREUX and VILLE Battery Establishment. No 13 Platoon Pioneers continued work in hand - BECOURT Platoon Redoubt.	

Army Form C. 2118

WAR DIARY
or
INTELLIGENCE SUMMARY
(Erase heading not required.)

9th Field Coy R.E. Sheet 5

Place	Date	Hour	Summary of Events and Information	Remarks and references to Appendices
DERNANCOURT	16.1.16 to 22.1.16		H.Q and No 2. Section. Sawing timber. The engine broke down on 17.1.16 and a new piston and rod had to be made in AMIENS. Making trench gratings. hand-troaeo. rifle grenade latrines. writ. boxes in village completed. No 1 Section working at TREUX. hutting under C.R.E. No 3 Section in D 3. 2 Steel shelters in 101 A and 101 B. 1 But & cover dugout in AVELVY. Stormchute line. Machine gun emplacements in head. Revetting and roofing dugouts in progress. 120 yards of Bonbril wire erected. No 4 Section in E 1. Bécourt Shelter dugout. Repairing 7 and 10 dugouts in Rubenhurst. Temporary propping and upkeeping two frames in dugout in BON ACCORD. Repairing timber of 3 dugouts — ABOYNE ST, DINET ST and bottom of SHUTTLE LANE. No 13 Platoon R. Sussex Pioneers working on BECOURT CHATEAU keep.	

Army Form C. 2118

WAR DIARY
or
INTELLIGENCE SUMMARY
(Erase heading not required.)

98' Field Co. R.E. Sheet 4

Place	Date	Hour	Summary of Events and Information	Remarks and references to Appendices
DERNANCOURT	23.1.16 to 31.1.16		H.Q. and No 4 Section. Repaired and reinstalled steam engine for Circular Saw. Work begun again 28.1.16. Making cement slabs, repairing billets, making cradles for Ponteins.	
			No 1 Section at TREUX hutting under C.R.E.	
			No 3 Section in D 3. Carrying on work as in previous week. Started laying gratings in the nullah from BÉCORDEL to MÉAULTE.	
			No 2 Section. Carrying on work as in previous week. Work on the three dugouts in the front line was abandoned owing to heavy shelling.	
			No 13 Platoon R. Sussex Pioneers. BECOURT CHATEAU Keep.	

R.E. Wright
Capt R.E.
for O.C. 92nd F. Co. R.E.

Army Form C. 2118

92 "Field Co R.E Sheet 5"

WAR DIARY
or
INTELLIGENCE SUMMARY
(Erase heading not required.)

Place	Date	Hour	Summary of Events and Information	Remarks and references to Appendices
			CASUALTIES for month of January 1916.	
	6.1.16.		Three Dismounted Reinforcements joined.	
	9.1.16.		1 Sapper evacuated sick.	
	16.1.16.		Major W.F. Lee R.E. handed over command of the Company to Captain J.A. Field R.E. 2 Drivers joined from 79th Coy 2 Drivers transferred to 79th Coy 1 Driver transferred to 18th Divn. H.Q. 9 Sappers sent home to Munition Workers. Two horses cast.	
	8.1.16.		Articles Requisitioned	
	12.1.16.		Roofing Tiles 516. For repair of billets in DERNANCOURT.	

R.S. Wright
Capt R.E
for O.C. 92nd Field Coy R.E.

War Diary
of
92nd Field Company R.E.
from 1st February
to 29th February 1916

Army Form C. 2118

WAR DIARY
or
INTELLIGENCE SUMMARY
(Erase heading not required.)

92nd Field Company R.E. Sheet 1

Place	Date	Hour	Summary of Events and Information	Remarks and references to Appendices
DERNANCOURT	1.2.16. to 7.2.16.		H.Q. and No.4 Section. Running Steam Saw – trench grating and shuttering. Making concrete slabs. Work on Dump at E end of village. Running carpenters shops.	
			No.2 Section relieved No.4 Section on the 5th. Work that date – work in E1 Château dugout completed. Dugout in SHUTTLE LANE route of DIVET ST. work on which had been stopped on 29.1.16. started again. Those in ABOYNE and DIVET ST. were abandoned definitely and work started on mining dugouts under the parapet. In the EMBANKMENT entrances widened to Nos. 7 and 10 dugouts, and work started on Nos. 8 and 10. Pumps tried out and water tested for analysis. The well in D3 was cleaned out, and a sample of water sent for analysis.	
			No.1 Section was relieved at TREUX by a section of the 95th F.Coy. R.E (7th Division) and started work at BUIRE (accommodation and water supply) under C.R.E.	
			No.3 Section handed over D3 Sector on 4th to 95th Coy. R.E. laid trench grating along water-course from BECORDEL to MEAULTE. This section moved out on the 6th en route for FLIXECOURT for duty at the 3rd Army Petrol.	
			No.13 Platoon R. Sussex Pioneers working in huts at BECOURT CHATEAU Redoubt.	

WAR DIARY or INTELLIGENCE SUMMARY

Army Form C. 2118

92nd Field Company R.E. Sheet 2

Place	Date	Hour	Summary of Events and Information	Remarks and references to Appendices
DERNANCOURT	8.2.16 to 14.2.16		H.Q. and No 2 Section. Running steam saw - making trench gratings, skating, and material for huts. Started work on Dump at E end of Railway - 50' of platform and 30 yards of road. Started work on huts for officers in Carpenters Shop. Platform started to erect Hung fell Ininometer in empty Barn in CANTERBURY St. 6th working in shops as required. Concrete slabs for lower top layers on emplacements. One Carpenter working in new gun position at 115th Battery R.G.A. Gun vestation post. D/85 R.F.A. No 1 Section. Fitter working on washing machine at VILLE Boiling Establishment. Remainder working at billet accommodation at BUIRE. No 3 Section - at 3rd Army School at FLIXECOURT. No 4 Section. Working in trenches on E. Continued work on mined dugouts in ABOYNE and DINET St. and steel shelter in SHUTTLE LANE. Bunting began on CHATEAU DUGOUT, and propping steel shelter. Bunting began on EMBANKMENT DUGOUTS and repairs to entrance. Roofing 4 dugouts in perimeter of BECOURT Redoubt. Repairs to dugout in BALMORAL St. to Regimental dugout left section. Revetting in ABERDEEN AVENUE.	

WAR DIARY
INTELLIGENCE SUMMARY

92nd Field Company R.E. Sheet 3

Army Form C. 2118

Place	Date	Hour	Summary of Events and Information	Remarks and references to Appendices
DERNANCOURT	15-2-16 to 21-2-16		H.Q. and No.2 Sections Running Steam saw, scantling and floorboarding for huts. Two large huts (20'x16' & 20'x10) made for Brigade. Also 10 small huts (10x8) made for 18th Divisional School. Horsfall Incinerator completed. Concrete slabs for bursting layers. One Sapper supervising work at Ville Balloon Section at VILLE. One Corporal supervising work at D/65 Gun positions. One Sapper supervising work at O.P. for 119th R.G.A. Work in shops as requisite. (b) No.1 Section. Working on beds at BUIRE and erecting machinery in VILLE Bathing establishment. Relieved No.4 in trenches on 19th. No.3 Section. Working at 3rd Army School at FLIXECOURT. No.4 Section. In E1 subsector. Continuation of 2 tunnelled dugouts ABOYNE and DINET. S.P. Repairs to dugout in BALMORAL ST. Bursting layers No.9 EMBANKMENT dugout. Centre propping from Shelters portion CHATEAU dugout. Beehive shelters in SHUTTLE LANE continued. Roofing dugouts round perimiter BECOURT Redoubt. Revetting ABERDEEN AVENUE. Repairing Signal dugout at left Company H.Q. Started 3 dugouts for M.O. near R.E. Dump. Started S.A.A. and Bomb Store in CHATEAU Yard. This section was relieved by No.1 in the trenches on 19th	

WAR DIARY
INTELLIGENCE SUMMARY

92nd Field Company R.E. Sheet 4

Army Form C. 2118

Place	Date	Hour	Summary of Events and Information	Remarks and references to Appendices
DERNANCOURT	22.2.16 to 29.2.16		H.Q. & No 2 Sect 2 running steam saws, Scantling & floorboarding for Div. School huts & hutment fireplaces. 7 small huts & 2 huts 10×8 erected for Div. School. Concrete slabs for mounting Vapors. 1 Sapper with Anti A.A. Bty R.G.A. making dugouts. No 1 Sect making beds in BUIRE & erecting machinery at N. VILLE Baths. No 3 Sect — at Army School FLIXECOURT. No 4 Sect. 2 C.E.1 section. The 2 tunnelled dug-outs 18×7' in firing line at ABOYNE & DINET streets practically finished. Beehive huts 15 (Chocolate ??) & Thatto lines finished & tunnelled annexe for signalling Set commenced. Old French dug out at 119 commenced the repairs & entrance cleared out. Officers dug-out in night of Buchan 57 strengthened. 5 dug outs 14 × 7 wind funnels of Becourt finished. Thato (another dug. Beehive shelter 2 heavy?? in follows no 9 line for Bomb stores 2. 18' long excavated for Medical during Feb. 1. 9' long for M.O. excavated & two dep. wants exits. Beds for 30. Machine Gunners put up in Becourt Chateau big dugout. 40 men of T.B. supplying trained rapid night mining. No 13 Platoon of E.R. Fusrs Pioneers finished Becourt Chateau Roof all except S.E. face. Capt Tyler went to 8 Gas E. School as instructor on 27th Feb.	

J. A. Davis
Capt R.E
O/C 92 Coy R.E
5/3/16

Army Form C. 2118

WAR DIARY
or
INTELLIGENCE SUMMARY

92ⁿᵈ Field Company R.E. Sheet 5

(Erase heading not required.)

Instructions regarding War Diaries and Intelligence Summaries are contained in F.S. Regs., Part II. and the Staff Manual respectively. Title Pages will be prepared in manuscript.

Place	Date	Hour	Summary of Events and Information	Remarks and references to Appendices
			Casualties for the month of February 1916	
DERNANCOURT	16-2-16		2 H.E. 0 + 1 Sapper evacuated	
	8-2-16		1 Sapper joined from 79th Field Company R.E.	
	31-1-16		10 Dismounted Reinforcements joined	
	14-2-16		1 Mounted Reinforcement joined	
	23-2-16		1 Mounted Reinforcement joined	
	8-2-16		1 N.C.O. Reinforcement joined	
	15-2-16		1 Sapper sent home as munition worker	
	19-2-16		1 Sapper sent to 32" (Base Park) Company R.E. in exchange	
			1 horse cast	

Gabriel Capt. R.E.
OC 92ⁿᵈ Field Company R.E.

War Diary
of
92ⁿᵈ Field Company R.E.
from 1-3-16
to 31-3-16

Capt. R.E.
OC 92nd (Fd.) Co. R.E.

WAR DIARY or INTELLIGENCE SUMMARY

Army Form C. 2118

92nd Field Co. R.E.   SHEET No 1

(Erase heading not required.)

Place	Date	Hour	Summary of Events and Information	Remarks and references to Appendices
FRECHENCOURT	1.3.16 to 7.3.16		All work in E. Subsector was handed over to 219th F.D Coy R.E.	
			On 3rd March Nos 2 and 4 Sections proceeded to FRECHENCOURT by march route.	
			" 4th March H.Q and No 1 Section " " " "	
			" 5th " Nos 2 and 4 and H.Q Carpenters proceeded to QUERRIEU and took over hutting etc. at 4th Army H.Q. These sections and carpenters	
			No 1 Section proceeded daily to the saw mill & place, felling trees and working them to the saw mill (which at present was not working owing to trouble with the engine (suction - gas plant)	
			1 Cpl and 3 men working on water supply system (postal engine and sup: well pump) at ALLONVILLE.	
			2 plumbers working at D.H.Q at MONTIGNY.	
			Capt. Tyler at 18th Divl School of Instruction.	
			No 3 Section at 3rd Army School at FLIXECOURT (hutting etc).	

Army Form C. 2118

92nd Field Co R.E.

Sheet No. 2

WAR DIARY
or
INTELLIGENCE SUMMARY
(Erase heading not required.)

Instructions regarding War Diaries and Intelligence Summaries are contained in F.S. Regs., Part II. and the Staff Manual respectively. Title Pages will be prepared in manuscript.

Place	Date	Hour	Summary of Events and Information	Remarks and references to Appendices
FRECHENCOURT	8/3/16 to 14/3/16		Nos 2 and 4 Sections and all other Carpenters working at QUERRIEU at 4th Army H.Q. erecting huts etc.	
	19/3/16		On 9/3/16 No 3 Section returned from FLIXECOURT.	
			H.Q. and Nos 1 and 3 Sections remained at FRECHEN COURT and undertook a refresher course of pontooning, rapid wiring etc. The Searchlights were also run.	
	18.3.16		The work at QUERRIEU was handed over to 202nd Fd Coy R.E. The following work had been carried out.	
			Small Map Hut 50' x 18'	
			Large Map Hut 156' x 18'	
			Batman's Mess Hut 50' x 11'	
			D.M.S. Mess Hut 46' x 14'	
			Dining Room Hut 62' x 17'	
			Floor for Garage 74' x 18'	
			2 Gunton Boilers	
			8 Latrines	
			also a considerable number of small jobs e.g. notice boards, erecting Armstrong Huts, tables, forms etc with interior work e.g. fitting stoves, windows, shelves, tables etc etc in various offices.	

WAR DIARY or INTELLIGENCE SUMMARY

92nd Field Co. R.E.

Sheet No 3

Army Form C. 2118

Place	Date	Hour	Summary of Events and Information	Remarks and references to Appendices
FRECHENCOURT	19.3.16		H.Q. and Nos 1 and 3 Section paraded at 9.30 a.m and marched to SAILLY-LE-SEC picking up Nos 2 and 4 Sections E of PONT NOYELLE. Arrived via CORBIE about 3 p.m. and went into Billets	
	20.3.16		Advanced party proceeded to BRAY to get the camp ready. Nos 1.3.4 Sections left at 2.30 p.m. and proceeded to SUZANNE via BRAY arriving at 6 p.m. H.Q. and No 2 Section paraded at 5 p.m and went into Camp at a point on the BRAY-ALBERT road 1000ˣ N of BRAY CHURCH arriving about 8 p.m.	
	21.3.16		The Company took on all work in Y1. Y2 and Y3 Sectors No 4 Section took over Y1 No 1 Section " " Y2 No 3 Section " " Y3 The work consisted chiefly in making dug outs, observation posts, machine gun emplacements etc etc A certain amount of work was required on the causeway leading from VAUX to KNOWLES POINT. in the way of screens and bridges.	

WAR DIARY or INTELLIGENCE SUMMARY

Army Form C. 2118

92nd Field Coy R.E.   Sheet No 4

Place	Date	Hour	Summary of Events and Information	Remarks and references to Appendices

BRAY & SUZANNE

21.3.16 to 31.3.16

Nos 4, 1 & 3 sections worked in Y.1, Y.2, Y.3 areas respectively.

Y.1 work. Collecting materials for ruined houses in VAUX village. 9 wooden picketa driven - 2 new hedge cradles & the side of indeep forest was river bridges were made. Snares were also revetted along causeway. The bridges over VAUX causeway were repaired. Breastwork with overhead cover over No 1 bridge 2/3 completed. A beehive 12' long erected. Tunnelled dug out joined up & completed behind old Coy. HQ. in Vaux. Dirk doven on pump which was blown up by shell. An O.P. made at D.84 R.7.a. A bridge put over SUZANNE avenue.

Y.2 Batt. H.Q. inside. No 18'6 beehive completed. No 2 tunnelled dug out 20' × 9' completed except for 2 frames. Holes dug out for another 18'6 beehive. 2 beds made to No 1 dug out.

Q.4 M.G. emp. completed except for frame. Narrow telephone trench put in position.

Q.2. dug out 16' × 9' (cut down) half completed. Ventilators begun.

Rayring fire dug out. Mines dug out 16' × 9' started - holes for 1.18 & 1.9 beehive.

1 bridge & trench made to W. Kents.

Y.3 5 beehive shelters (12'long) & corner of Beads St 3/4 completed. 5 entrances shelters 22'6" × 9' & Peuquoy road being started.

Dugout & 14 F.T. centre propped & finished. 15'amp 13' × 7' nearly finished. Telephone trench & 18'amp needs painting. Telephone room 6' × 6'. This shaft nearly finished. Dugout & shaft & 14'amp 15' × 7' nearly completed.

2 tunnelled dugouts at Bengalt 25' × 9' & 30 × 9 which were unfinished, shewed falls in, were started again. 1 new entrance shelter 48 × 8' in Bengalt has had repairs begun on it.

No 2 sec. & H.Q. & B.O.S. workshop worked on water supply, hand plates, wooden bowls, making 2 loopholes, 2 knife-rests, 1 latrine screen, working workshop chiefly sawn benches.

Army Form C. 2118

92nd Field Co. R.E.   Sheet No 5

WAR DIARY
or
INTELLIGENCE SUMMARY
(Erase heading not required.)

Place	Date	Hour	Summary of Events and Information	Remarks and references to Appendices
BRAY and SUZANNE	27/2/16 to 3/3/16		H.Q. and No 2 Section. Took over workshops at CHIPILLY. Removed saw bench from windmills at ETINHEM, and erected it there. Sent new will shaft alongside Ramp near the R.E. Park, and installed Evinrude Motor Pump. Capt. Tyler and 6 O.R. detailed for duty at 18th Divisional School at LA HOUSSOIE.	

R.S. Wright
Capt R.E.
for O.C. 92nd F.Co. R.E.

WAR DIARY or INTELLIGENCE SUMMARY

Army Form C. 2118

92nd Field Coy RE

Sheet No 6

Place	Date	Hour	Summary of Events and Information	Remarks and references to Appendices
BRAY.	1/3/16 to 31/3/16		Casualties during month of March 1916.	
	14.3.16		1 Dismounted Reinforcement joined.	

R.F. Wright
Cap.t R.E.
for
O.C. 92nd F.Coy R.E.

Secret

War Diary of
92ⁿᵈ Field Co RE

from 1/4/16
to 30/4/16

[signature]
Captain RE
OC 92ⁿᵈ Field Co RE

WAR DIARY or INTELLIGENCE SUMMARY

Army Form C. 2118

92nd Field Co. R.E.

Sheet No. 1

Place	Date	Hour	Summary of Events and Information	Remarks and references to Appendices
BRAY and SUZANNE	1/4/16 to 7/4/16		H.Q and No 2 Section. Running saw Mills at CHIPILLY and R.E. Works lot at BRAY whence chevaux de frise, trench latrine covers, rifle grenade batteries etc. Making water supply for horses near R.E. Park. No 4 Section working in Y. Sector. (a) Galvin Breastwork completed 90' long. (b) Gun post on Causeway completed. (c) Bridges at Duchess post completed. (d) 18' Bridge entrance to Causeway started. (e) Bridges on Causeway completed. (f) Breastwork apron (g) Latrines (h) Forced point for water supply. (i) 2 Bridge communication trench to Road (j) Built bridge on causeway post bridge past FRISE point. (k) Work on 2nd entrance to VAUX Mine (l) Work on well in valley. (m) Breastwork mines at SUZANNE bridge. (n) Beds for SUZE R.E. Dressing Station. No 1 Section working in Y2 Sector. (a) No 2 Mine Dugout 20' × 9' completed. (b) No 3 Mine Dugout 2 frames erected. (c) No 1 Mine Dugout strengthened. (d) Q2 Dugout 16' × 8' almost completed. Q4 Magazine emplacement completed. FARGNY MILL Mine Dugout Q1, M.Gun emplacement started. excavation started 2 entrances 12' driven. (2) Beehive in Y3 in lot 14 completed. (3) 9' Beehive statework completed. No 3 Section working in Y3 5 Beehives 12' long completed. Dugout 15" × 5' in lot 14 completed. 2 Mined Dugouts DEAN'S GATE ST Edmund chot at 2 River dugout. Running dugouts Browns dugouts 5 half finished and a sath started. Making loles for "Dog Kennel" shelters in fire trench.	

WAR DIARY or INTELLIGENCE SUMMARY

Army Form C. 2118

9th Field Coy R.E.

Sheet No 2

Place	Date	Hour	Summary of Events and Information	Remarks and references to Appendices
BRAY and SUZANNE	8/4/16 to 12/4/16		H.Q. and No 2 Section. Saw Mills at CHIPILLY and B.th Workshop at BRAY Water Supply Scheme to BOIS DES TAILLES. No 2 Section relieved by No 4 12/4/16	
	12/4/16		No 4 Section in Y1 Sector (Relieved by No 1 on 12/4/16.) (a) 1 Main post on VAUX Causeway & complete. (b) Temporary bridge at lock on Causeway dismantled, and piling begun for new bridge. (c) New exit to mine carried on. (d) Work on well 18' gone. Iron bridges made for Causeway. No 1 Section in Y2 Sector (Relieved by No 2 on 12/4/16. (a) No 3 Dugout. HQ Reserve completed and B.O's Dugout centre propped. Q2 Dugout completed. (b) Q1 M.G. Emp'. Placement slewing drains and revetted. (c) FARGNY MILL. Shaft dugout 16 x 9' started 9' Beehive completed. 18' Beehive Eight elements fixed. No 3 Section in Y3 Sector. 2 Dugouts (25'x5' and 30'x5') in DEANSGATE completed. Cut-2 Crown Dugout 48'x 9' Completed except Bunks. Large Ramie Pillbox 22' 6" x 5' new ones completed and erection of beds begun. Four nearly completed. Two completed and one first started. Latrine started. Capt Tyler and 6 O.R returned from LA HOUSSOIE from attachment at 18th Divl School.	
	12/4/16		Work in B Sector Four entrances to dug-outs excavated and tunnel Entrances to Parapelles dugouts commenced Work in A2 30 R.A.M.C. attached working on MARICOURT R.D.	

WAR DIARY or INTELLIGENCE SUMMARY

Army Form C. 2118

92 Field Coy RE   Sheet No 3

Place	Date	Hour	Summary of Events and Information	Remarks and references to Appendices
BRAY and SUZANNE	15/4/16		H.Q. and No.4 Section Saw Mills at CHIPILLY and Brigade Workshops at BRAY. Water Supply Scheme in BOIS DES TAILLES and BRAY.	
	23/4/16		No 1 Section in Y. Sector 5 6in M.G. ports in causeway complete. Spare No.4 Bridge finished. from slating for Bridge. New exit to VAUX mine complete 30' wide on S side of No 3 Dugout in DRAGON'S WOOD 16x8' new exit to well - depth 65 ft.	
			No 2 Section in Y2 Platoon Hut erected in Q.1. Infantry 2 not finished. Left down from shaft to face of dugout. 3 FARGNY MILL dugouts complete + inspectrin. consol ST Dugout 5x6 started. M.G. emplacement - Headquarters	
			No 3 Section in Y3 and Copse B. In Y3 Ronny Pilton St. holes erected for B. Copse Pilot leading driven widened and 16 frames fixed. finale dugout - entrance driven dugout excavated and all frames fixed.	
			Work in A.2. Preparation of working party in LEEDS AVENUE grading and cleaning out. Laid out 300 yards new track from junction RATTY & RATTY to QUEENS also town track from junction COKE & MURCHISTON to SUNK Rd. Completed new bridge over trench w of MARICOURT by OXFORD COPSE	

Army Form C. 2118

WAR DIARY
or
INTELLIGENCE SUMMARY
(Erase heading not required.)

9th Field Co R.E. Sheet No 4

Place	Date	Hour	Summary of Events and Information	Remarks and references to Appendices
BRAY + SUZANNE	22/4/16 to 30/4/16		No 1 Section in Y/1 sector. This Section moved from SUZANNE to B.Copse 30/4/16. 1 one man post on CRUSEVRAY finished (6 completed during month). Above 20 additional piles at No 3 bridge, revetted banks, strutted and cross braced piers. Made good new entrance to VAUX mine, and fitted anti gas doors to both entrances. Indians beds in VAUX mine 1h completed. Continued work on well, struck water 25/4/16 depth to water 41ft total depth 44ft. Completed 16'x 8' dugout in DRAGONS WOOD. No 3 Section in Y/3 sector & B.Copse. No 3 Section moved to BRAY 30/4/16. Y2. Ravine Shelters. Five completed, four fitted with beds, two others nearly completed. Latrine made. DEANS GATE. dugout 48'x 9'. Two feet earth put on roof. 300 concrete slabs sent to Battalion for bursting layer. Left-Bay W. Gas. Repairs to roof which was blown in by a shell. B.Copse only two more frames to fix in west dugout, others completed except for revetting sides and centre proppings. No 2 Section in Y/2 sector and B. Copse. No 2 Section marched to QUERRIEU 28/4/16. dugout in CONSUL STREET 9'x 6'. Completed and fitted with beds. Second entrance to open ground at back remains to be tunnelled. Q1 M.G. emplacement- completed except for insertion of Coophole, and frame of table. B.Copse. Revetting sides of Signal dugout. Water supply:- excavated 12'x 9' temporary tinhouse, floors of roof frames + supply pipes + tanks, excavating stairway + revetting sides. HQ and No 4 section B. Carpenters with Amn 28/4/16 Water supply. Schemes saw Mills at CHIPILLY BOIS DES TAILLES and BRAY. J.W.A Captain RE O.C. 9th Field Co RE	

1875 Wt. W593/826 1,000,000 4/15 J.B.C. & A. A.D.S.S./Forms/C.2118.

WAR DIARY
or
INTELLIGENCE SUMMARY

92nd Field Co. R.E.   Sheet No. 5

Army Form C. 2118

Place	Date	Hour	Summary of Events and Information	Remarks and references to Appendices
BRAY			Casualties during month of April 1916	
	1-4-16 to 30-4-16			
	1-4-16		1. N.C.O. reinforcement joined	
	19-4-16		2 N.B.Os & 7 ORs transferred to 19th Gen Base Depot on reduction of establishment through withdrawal of Oxy carry time personnel from field companies	
	21-4-16		1 O.R. admitted to Hospital	
	28-4-16		1 O.R. proceeded to S.O. Cavalry Reinforcement for transfer to England	
	29-4-16		1 O.R. admitted to Hospital	
	14-4-16		1 horse destroyed through injury to foot — Articles requisitioned	
	24-4-16		1 4 H.P. National Petrol engine for use on water supply in BRAY	

J. Morris Captain R.E.
O.C. 92nd Field Co R.E.

Army Form C. 2118

WAR DIARY
or
INTELLIGENCE SUMMARY
(Erase heading not required.)

XVIII   VOL 10.

92ⁿᵈ Field Coy RE   SHEET - 1

Instructions regarding War Diaries and Intelligence Summaries are contained in F.S. Regs., Part II. and the Staff Manual respectively. Title Pages will be prepared in manuscript.

Place	Date	Hour	Summary of Events and Information	Remarks and references to Appendices
BRAY	1/5/16 to 7/5/16		H.Q and No 3 Section Running Saw Mills at CHIPILLY. Water Supply to BOIS DES TAILLES completed except for minor fittings. Water Supply in BRAY continued. No 1 Section living in B before - working in A, sites (a) Tunnel under PERONNE Rᵈ on Trench No 6. Entrance on S side of Trench No 5. Bridge over Nº5 trench started. (c) Revetting entrance to dugout B (d) Collecting station at junction of COKE and MERCHISTON. One finished, now dug. (e) Put in 2 Platoon Shelters in BILLON VALLEY. (f) Taped out 670 yards of firing & trenches in A₁ - A₂ and 520 yards communication trench in rear. This section moved to BILLON WOOD 7/5/16. No 4 Section 1/5/16 - 3/5/16 work with H.Q. on water supplies. 4/5/16 - 7/5/16 excavating and building two 26' shelters in BILLON VALLEY. No 2 Section at 4ᵗʰ Army H.Q. at QUERRIEU - work as reported in officers letters etc.	
	6/5/16 to 14/5/16		H.Q and No 3 Section Running Saw Mills at CHIPILLY. Working of Water Supply to BOIS DES TAILLES until 12/5/16 when it was handed over to The Adjutant 16ᵗʰ Divisional Engineers. Water supply in BRAY continued	

Army Form C. 2118

WAR DIARY
or
INTELLIGENCE SUMMARY
(Erase heading not required.)

9² Field Co R.E.

Sheet 2

Place	Date	Hour	Summary of Events and Information	Remarks and references to Appendices
BRAY	8/5/16 to 14/5/16		**No 1 Section** Tunnel under PERONNE R⁴ completed accept for exit. Work continued on collecting Stations four days, two roofed. Bridge over No 5 trench completed. Started roofing 20'x 9' dugout RAIL AVENUE. Roofed 9'x 8' Headquarter dugout in PRINCES ST. Repaired bridge across SHEFFIELD AVENUE. Working on Brigade H'Qrs. moved dugout BILLON VALLEY. 460 x 2" line formers up trench QUEEN ST to MARY ST dug 3'6" wide 6" deep and 240' 3rd line taped. **No 2 Section** at 4th Army H.Qrs at QUERRIEU. Work as requisite in offices, billets, etc. moved to PICQUIGNY for work on saw bench and necessary work required for under 18th division 9/5/16 **No 4 Section** Training in technical work at CHIPILLY from 9/5/16 to 18/5/16.	
	15.5.16 to 28.5.16		**Hq & No. 3 Section** Running saw mills at CHIPILLY. Working on water supply BOIS DES TAILLES. Working at 18th Div. Dump. Working on new dugouts at 92nd R.E. H.Q. **No. 1 Section** Training in technical work at CHIPILLY from 18.5.16 to 28.5.16. **No. 2 Section** Working at 18 Div. H.Q. PICQUIGNY. Timber cutting, improving camp accommodation, laying out and supervising digging of 7 miles French	

WAR DIARY
or
INTELLIGENCE SUMMARY

(Erase heading not required.)

92ⁿᵈ Field Co RE   Sheet 3

Place	Date	Hour	Summary of Events and Information	Remarks and references to Appendices
BRAY	16.5.16 to 25.5.16		No 4 Section: BILLON VALLEY. Mining new Bde. Hqs. Putting beds into existing dugouts. PERONNE Rd. Finishing tunnel under Water. Work on collecting station in A1. sector. Laying out and spitlocking new forward trenches. Trench Mortar position. Dugouts for Co. Hq. etc. in A1. under construction.	
	26/5/16 to 31/5/16		No 1 & No 2 Sections Running saw bench at CHIPILLY. Workers at 18ᵗʰ Divisional dump BRAY. Improving old and building new dugouts at Hqᵣˢ 92ⁿᵈ Co RE No 3 Section Training in technical work at CHIPILLY from 26/5/16 relieved No 1 on the same date. No 2 Section Workers at 18ᵗʰ Divisional Headquarters. PICQUIGNY. Improving camp accommodation, working saw bench, repairs and improvm'ts Anti gas school, and improving old line of defences No 4 Section Mining new Bde Hqʳˢ dug out continued, erecting beds in dugouts in BILLON VALLEY. Repairing water supply for 8ᵗʰ Sussex Pioneers. Completing revetting of tunnel under PERONNE road at trench 5. Continuing work on dressing stations, junction of MANCHESTER & LEEDS AVENUES. A dugout of RAIL AVENUE nearly complete. Work on trench mortar position off MARY "S.7".	

M__
Captain RE
OC 92ⁿᵈ Field Co RE

Army Form C. 2118

WAR DIARY
or
INTELLIGENCE SUMMARY

(Erase heading not required.)

92ⁿᵈ Field Co. R.E.   Sheet 4

Instructions regarding War Diaries and Intelligence Summaries are contained in F.S. Regs., Part II. and the Staff Manual respectively. Title Pages will be prepared in manuscript.

Place	Date	Hour	Summary of Events and Information	Remarks and references to Appendices
BRAY	1/5/16 to 31/5/16		Casualties during month of May 1916	
	1/5/16		1. O.R transferred to 235ᵗʰ A.T. Coy RE	
	6/5/16		1. O.R evacuated to No 21 C.C.S	
			2. O.R admitted to Hospital. one evacuated out of 18ᵗʰ Divisional area	
	13/5/16		Capt Wright RE transferred to 200ᵗʰ Field Co RE	
			2. drivers transferred to 200ᵗʰ Field Co RE	
			2. drivers transferred from 200ᵗʰ Co RE to 92ⁿᵈ Co RE	
	13/5/16		1. officer struck off strength of 92ⁿᵈ Field Co RE (not fit for general service)	
	24/5/16		1. officer arrived from France (reinforcement)	
	29/5/16		1. officer " "	
			1. Horse cast	

J. Gavin
Captain R.E.
O.C. 92ⁿᵈ Field Co R.E.

WAR DIARY or INTELLIGENCE SUMMARY

Army Form C. 2118.

Place	Date	Hour	Summary of Events and Information	Remarks and references to Appendices
BURBURE	1.5.1916		Route March. Drills & fatigues.	
	2		Drills, Working Parade & fatigues.	
	3		Route march, Drills & fatigues.	
	4		Drill. Shorts of 33rd Divn.	
	5		Route march & fatigues.	
	6		Drill & fatigues.	
	7 Sunday		Fatigues. Nil Divisional parade owing to rain.	
MAROC	8		Company moved to MAROC. Dismounted Started. mounted returned.	
	9		Fatigues & billets. Setting out works at FOSSE 7. Taking of Bde Engs. NCO Reconn-
	10		M.G. Emplacements. Dugouts, wiring, digging, trench & trench End.R.T. Divs.the
	11		" " " " Rivers traverble
	12/13		Qs on the 10th " " " Bench into stretch trench.
	14		" " 10 " " "
	15		" " " " "
	16		" " " " " Lt. Col. Knox relinquished command of 7th Divisional date of Feb 8 Sec.
BURBURE	17/18		" " " " to Lt. Col. Knox relinquished rest billets at BURBURE
	19		Company moved from MAROC into rest billets at BURBURE.	
	20/21		Drills & fatigues.	
	22		4 Sections with 1st Fort Garage cars moved to COYECQUE for work in entrenchments
	23		H. Army Menage Bre. No. 6. 155 Section remained at BURBURE.
	24		4 Sections on entrenchments on COYECQUE. F. S. A. at Burbure. Kit inspection
COYECQUE	25		ditto. Divisional service Parade. Divisional inspection.
	26		H.B. moved to COYECQUE. I NCO 7 ORs Lt.nyt. horse & battle Waggon to HPQT Division.

A. Darling Capt. R.E.
Commanding 69th (FIELD) COMPANY R.E.

Army Form C. 2118.

WAR DIARY
or
INTELLIGENCE SUMMARY.

(Erase heading not required.)

Instructions regarding War Diaries and Intelligence Summaries are contained in F. S. Regs., Part II. and the Staff Manual respectively. Title pages will be prepared in manuscript.

Place	Date	Hour	Summary of Events and Information	Remarks and references to Appendices
COYECQUE	27.	5.16.	4 Sections in entrenchments. Orders received at 7.45 P.M. to move at once to BURBURE. Company marched out and arrived at BURBURE at 8.20 A.M. 28.5.16.	
BURBURE	28.		Resting. Drills. "Standing to" from 11.a.m. To move at 1 hours notice.	
"	29		" " " " To move at 1 hours notice.	
"	30		" " " " To move at 1 hours notice.	
"	31		" " " " To move at 2 hours notice during night & housed during day.	

J. Dowling
Capt. R.E.
COMMANDING 69th (FIELD) COMPANY R.E.

92 FCRE
Vol II
June

XVIII

SECRET

War Diary of
    92 Field Company RE

from
    1-6-16
to
    30-6-16

[signature] Captain RE
for OC 92 Field Co RE

WAR DIARY or INTELLIGENCE SUMMARY

Army Form C. 2118

92ⁿᵈ Field Coy RE

Place	Date	Hour	Summary of Events and Information	Remarks and references to Appendices
BRAY	1/6/16		Hd Qrs + No 1 Sections	
			Painting and lettering notice boards for advance trenches, started making dugout 8' x 10' on Gravelcum Camp. Loading and checking RE material sent from 18th Divisional Dump to advance dumps, supplying Draftsman and guides for same. Two men employed at 18th Divisional dump on technical work. working parties found at CHIPILLY making Chevaux-de-frise. Repairing company transport.	
			Nº 2 Section	
			Harassing work at 18th Division Hd Qrs at PICQUIGNY. 1/6/16 moved to Rest Camp CHIPILLY 5th and training in defensive work	
			Nº 3 Section	
			Technical work at Rest Camp CHIPILLY from 1st to 5th marched to BILLON VALLEY commenced making Bussing station dugout in Rail Avenue. Started new tunnelled dugout 33' x 8'. Commenced tunnellers old tunnel under PERONNE road. Took over tunnelled 88' x 9' dugout in BILLON VALLEY	
			Nº 4 Section	
	8/6/16		Dressing stations continued, fitted with beds and stretcher racks & now completed. Some nearly completed	
			2'4" x 4'6" Trench mortar position in many Street completed 2 T.m positions in George Street started + one in Queen Street started. Mined dugout in BILLON VALLEY continued under 6 ft. when it is handed over to Nº 3 Section	

WAR DIARY
or
INTELLIGENCE SUMMARY

(Erase heading not required.)

Army Form C. 2118.

92nd Field Co RE   Sheet No 2

Place	Date	Hour	Summary of Events and Information	Remarks and references to Appendices
BRAY	6/6/16 to 19/6/16		No 4 Section continued one mined dugout off Rail avenue. Continued Rail avenue dump. French duggins and Bayonet ave. making latrines, sump pit etc for the section.	
			4th Aus + No 1 Sections	
			Painting and Lettering notice boards for advance dumps and trenches, making dugout in Grovetown Camp 24'x9' partly completed, loading and checking RE material sent to advance trenches + dumps supplying guides and foreman for same. Five men employed upon technical work at 18th Divl. dump. Running engine at CHIPILLY saw bench, repairing engine and Recoupe plant in running order. Making 200 trench "pull ups" preparing iron pickets for chevaux-de-frize. Making bomb boxes.	
			No 2 Section	
			Technical work at CHIPILLY until 12th. moved to BRAY on 13th. Company employed with this Co until 15th on evening of 15th proceeded to the trenches in A section and worked under Lieut Knight. O.C No 4 Section.	
			No 3 Section	
			Continued work on mined dugout in BILLON VALLEY. 20'x8' also dugout in RAIL valley, commenced widening bridges over Sheffield & Bedford (up) to 12' wide. finished supervising two bays of 1st R.W Kent Ryl in digging by day and night. Bedford trench	

Army Form C. 2118.

WAR DIARY
or
INTELLIGENCE SUMMARY
(Erase heading not required.)

92" field Co. RE

Sheet N° 3.

Place	Date	Hour	Summary of Events and Information	Remarks and references to Appendices
BRAY	8/6/16 to 19/6/16		N° 3 Section continued. Continued work on dressing station Rail Avenue and handed over on 19.F. completely roofed, two window openings, sandbagged and west side revetted, propped up railway where it crosses Bedford & Sheffield, finished. Roofing bomb stores dump & revetting, etc finished. Received gratings in Sheffield avenue, Roofing bomb stores 5 off. 15'×9'. 3 finished. Rail avenue and Mined dugout in Billon Valley, and material handed over to Lieut Wadeson OC N° 1 Section 19.F on the same date marched into Cos. H.Q. N° 4 Section. Superintending digging of and laying out of new lines. Completion of mined dugout Pongaste. Bomb stores begins, out-digging of and roofing started. Letting in tanks for the Reserve of water, fitting tanks on trucks, and working on collecting stations. Right Pole dump Card aut. Bomb store top of Gold Avenue started, mine continued work on T.M. positions in Gorge, Queens, + Many struts. Refining by N° 2 Section on 15.F. N° 1, 2, 3, + 4 Sections.	
BRAY	18/6/16 to 30/6/16		N° 1 Section relieved N° 3 in BILLON VALLEY 19/6/16. N° 3 section relieved N° 2 at CARNOY 24/6/16. N° 2 + 4 sections proceeded to trenches 29/6/16. N° 1 section arrived BRAY 29/6/16	

Army Form C. 2118.

WAR DIARY
or
INTELLIGENCE SUMMARY
(Erase heading not required.)

Instructions regarding War Diaries and Intelligence Summaries are contained in F. S. Regs., Part II and the Staff Manual respectively. Title Pages will be prepared in manuscript.

92nd Field Co. R.E.

Sheet N° 4

Place	Date	Hour	Summary of Events and Information	Remarks and references to Appendices
BRAY			Putting in points, sidings on Railway, preparing rails, sleepers etc for 400 yards new track.	
			Makers water trenches, preparing advance dumps for Conk stores, finished.	
			Completed mined signal dugout in BILLON VALLEY 25'x9'. Started two dugouts in RAIL AVENUE 25'x9' and 31'x9' one finished. Four trench mortar pits completed. Two advanced dumps in front line one BATTY road one COKE AVENUE completed. Cook house 12'x9'x6' finished. completed shelter for R.A.M.B. in Rail AVENUE. Superimposed wagons of trench from MERCHISTON AVENUE to R.A.M.E shelter.	
			Headquarters Section	
			Workers on dugouts for bay. workers on divisional dump. made 350 trench pull ups. making tools for railway sleepers etc. loading on an average 10 wagons nightly with R.E material for advanced dumps. making and painting 350 notice boards. making trench gratings	

M.J.R. Captain R.E.
for O.C. 92. Field Co R.E.

Army Form C. 2118.

WAR DIARY
or
INTELLIGENCE SUMMARY

(Erase heading not required.)

92 Field Co RE Sheet No 5

Place	Date	Hour	Summary of Events and Information	Remarks and references to Appendices
BRAY	1/6/16 to 30/6/16		Casualties during month of June 1916	
			1 O.R. transferred to 49th Field Co RE	
			2 N.C.Os + 4 O.R. transferred to England for work on munitions	
			1 Officer transferred to 80th Field Co RE	
			2 Officers joined from Base (Reinforcements)	
			1 N.C.O 1 O.R. admitted to Hospital (sick)	
			One officer joined 92 Co RE on transfer from 80th Co RE	
			1. wounded O.R. joined from Base (Reinforcement)	
			1 O.R. killed in action	
			2 O.R. admitted to Hospital wounded	
			2 L.D and 2 riders joined	

[signature] Captain RE
for OC 92 Field Coy RE

18/Vol 12

92ND FIELD COMPANY, R.E.

Headquarters.
18º Division.

Herewith War diary of the 92nd Field Company RE for July 1916.

B Chambers Capt RE
† Colonel
C.R.E., 18º Division

4.8.16.

Army Form C. 2118.

WAR DIARY
or
INTELLIGENCE SUMMARY
(Erase heading not required.)

92nd Duke of R.E.   Sheet 1

Place	Date	Hour	Summary of Events and Information	Remarks and references to Appendices
CARNOY	1/7/16	9.30a.m.	No 4 Section under Lieut Knight RE proceeded up to R.E.H.Q. report centre with one platoon of 9th Buffs for carrying. On arrival at right report centre a shelf tree in the maitre Trenching out 4 Sappers, the officer and some men of the Buffs. This rather disorganised matters at the time.	
		10.30a.m.	Proceeded forward and commenced to consolidate strong points A. 3. c. 29. Where consolidating, the section was not much troubled by shellfire at first. The carrying party seems to be losing its officer lost its way getting to the point, and after that they did not carry too well. Went, the steps M.G. emplacements and loop holes were carried out.	
		9.30 a.m	No 2 Section under Lieut Nunn R.E. moved up from RAIL AVENUE with one platoon of 8th R.S. Pioneers	
		1.15 A.M.	Crossed over front line and proceeded with Pioneers to MONTAUBAN. Arrived 2:15 P.M. Lieut Nunn then reconnoitred the point he had to consolidate viz the two western houses of MONTAUBAN. 2.Lieut Young (Pioneers) then commenced to consolidate the two points allotted him viz. S.24 c.6.6 + S.24.c.3.6. Work was then carried on under shell and M.G. fire till 2.30.a.m. except for an interval of 2 hours (8.30 to 10.30 p.m.) when the section was ordered to stand to in anticipation of an attack. Loop holes and dug-in could mostly be done by day, but it was necessary to do the work by night. This section luckily only suffered 5 casualties (all wounded) of which occurred before leaving our lines. Section returned to CARNOY (RAIL AVENUE) at 5.A.M arrives 7 A.M 2/7/16	
		8. a.m	No 1 Section under Lieut Wadeson marched from BRAY, arrived RAIL AVENUE 9.45 a.m. at 8 p.m the section marched out to	

Army Form C. 2118.

WAR DIARY
or
INTELLIGENCE SUMMARY
(Erase heading not required.)

92nd Field Co RE   Sheet 2.

Place	Date	Hour	Summary of Events and Information	Remarks and references to Appendices
CARNOY	1/4/16		No 1 section continued POMMIER LINE and relieved No 4 section at 9 p.m. The section tried to wire but did not do much owing to heavy shelling. 3 casualties were suffered. No 3 Section under 2nd Lieut Beattie	
		9.30 A	started loading up trucks with railway material at 9.30 am and moved off to repair the railway while loading up at dump one sapper got wounded by spent bullet, while rushing up trucks another got wounded while working forward the section got a shell in the midst of them killed four of the working party and 1 sapper wounded about 6 including 2/Lieut Beattie. after this the 2nd Corpl. left in charge reported to O.C. who on receiving the message at 2.15 p.m. told them to return.	
		12.45 P.M. and 2.R	I telephoned to 55th Bde and asked them for carrying parties for No 2 sec. but they were unable to supply me with them. at 2.50 p.m. received G.R.E.'s message telling me to fill in road along railway and to help R.A. coming along so obtained limbers from Sussex Pioneers who did this work out and inspected work done on POMMIER LINE and on MILL TRENCH	
		5.30 P.M.	about 12 midnight 3 bays belonging to 9th Division arrived to take up stores these were given loads and guided up to MONTAUBAN they got shelled on the way and deposited most of their stuff in MILL TRENCH.	
	2/4/16		No 1 Section relieved on the POMMIER LINE work by No 4 section at 11 a.m. This section practically completed the wiring etc of these strong points, and returned to RAIL AVE in the afternoon.	

Army Form C. 2118.

WAR DIARY
or
INTELLIGENCE SUMMARY

(Erase heading not required.)

92- Sheet 30 NE   Sheet 3

Place	Date	Hour	Summary of Events and Information	Remarks and references to Appendices
CARNOY	2/4/16	8.a.m	**N° 2 Section** Marched out and wired in front of our front line along MONTAUBAN ALLEY putting up 300 yards. Section returned about 3 a.m 3/4/16. **N° 4 Section** Finished work on POMMIER LINE. 3 water tanks were put in just S. of Pommier Line and 2 on BRESLAU SUPPORT both places on the MONTAUBAN ROAD. **N° 3 Section** Repaired broken wires of the railway line	
	3/4/16		N° 1 and 4 sections worked in MONTAUBAN ALLEY by day revetting trench and vaulting up traverses. N° 3 Section and platoon of Pioneers (9th Division) worked on the road and railway. The two water points on Montauban Road finished off today. A crossing made across the Railway at TALUS BOISE so as to help the R.A. coming from S of our area.	
	4/4/16		**N° 1 Section** constructed 3 road bridges at CARNOY, TALUS BOISE, and MONTAUBAN in old german line and supervised one Coy of Infantry in filling in shell holes and making track. **N° 2 + 4 Sections** Improving trenches MONTAUBAN ALLEY. **N° 3 Section** [illegible] RAIL Avenue as new aid post in VALLEY SUPPORT	

WAR DIARY or INTELLIGENCE SUMMARY

Army Form C. 2118.

(Erase heading not required.)

Place	Date	Hour	Summary of Events and Information	Remarks and references to Appendices
CARNOY	4/7/16		Church, assisted by two platoons of Pioneers (9th Bn) installed 3 tanks and experimental profile same at Aid Post. Railway opened to Skoffle H.P.M.	
"	5.7.16		Standpipe fixed at junction of Train Alley & Railway. Was strengthening with wire entanglements. TALUS BOISÉ Valley track was completed through to outskirts of MONTAUBAN. Prisoners of 9th Bn. 2 camouflets 120'×22' were constructed at BRONFAY farm. Repairs to railway wire gone on with.	
BRAY	6.7.16		No 2 section constructed a hut 60'×20' at BRONFAY. No 1.3+4 sections returned to Headquarters at BRAY & commenced constructing shelters for 8th East Surrey Regt at BRAY. one 120'×28" two 140'×44'	
"	7/7/16		No 3 section continued work on East Surrey Camp. Nos 2+4 sections off duty during morning afternoon period out hutments for 53rd Infantry Brigade (L. 9. a. 9.1)	
"	8/7/16		Handed over forward work near MONTAUBAN to East Riding Field Coy RE 3rd Division All company continued erecting hutments for 53rd Bde. one 84'×28 two 100'×20' + two 24'×24' finished	
"	9/7/16 10/7/16		No 3 section continued work on shelters for East Surrey. Nos 1-2+4 sections day off No 1 section improving road from BRONFAY to CARNOY. No 2. section repairs and alterations to water supply at L. 9. c. 9.5	
"	11/7/16		No 2 section continued work on water supply, No 1 section continued work on road No 4 repairing road BRONFAY - CARNOY between F.18.c.5.3 and CARNOY	
"	12/7/16		No 2 section continued work on water supply No 3 section work on road No 4 section made a bridge on BRONFAY - CARNOY Road F.18.c.5.3	

Army Form C. 2118.

WAR DIARY
or
INTELLIGENCE SUMMARY

(Erase heading not required.)

Instructions regarding War Diaries and Intelligence Summaries are contained in F. S. Regs., Part II. and the Staff Manual respectively. Title Pages will be prepared in manuscript.

Place	Date	Hour	Summary of Events and Information	Remarks and references to Appendices
BRAY	12/7/16	7.30 A.M.	Commanders officer with Nos 2, 3 & 4 sections proceeded to COPSE VALLEY A.2.Y.8. and relieved 200th Field Co.RE 30th Division	
COPSE VALLEY	13 & 14/7/16	5.15pm	Headquarter section installed new pump in BRAY water supply. Nos 2 & 4 sections arrived forward dump 4 pm. Loaded themselves with RE material and went forward to consolidate at S.20.A.5.4. arriving there at 11.30am. whom points were consolidated at S.20.A.5.4. & S.24.c.2.2. Captain J.A Field Officer Commanding Company was killed while going up with these sections. Nos 1 & 3 sections relieved Nos 2 & 4 at 12 midday. the latter returning to BRAY during afternoon. Nos 1 & 3 sections started to consolidate two points viz S.30.A.5.4 & S.30.A.9.5 very little work could be done on account of snipers and had to be abandoned. The two sections returned at 9 pm. and returned to COPSE VALLEY arriving 1 am 15/7/16. men were fed and taken to BRAY on pontoon wagons	
BRAY	15/7/16 to 17/7/16		All sections resting except for inspections, and drill. Running water supplies at (1) BRAY Railway Station (2) GROVE TOWN.	
	18/7/16		No 1 Sect began erection of new Dn.l.H.Q. at MINDEN POST F.18.c.	
	20/7/16		All by transport left BRAY at 3.45 pm by road, arrived ALLONVILLE 12 midnight. Bivouacked in overcoat.	
	21/7/16		Transport left ALLONVILLE 8.30 am, arriving HOCQUINCOURT 5.30 pm. Dismounted branch under O.C. left BRAY at 8 am. Entrained at MERICOURT 11.30 am. Detrained at LONGPRE les Corps Saints 4.30pm. Marched to HOCQUINCOURT arriving 6.15 pm. Rest Coy in billets. Remainder in Bivouacs.	

Army Form C. 2118.

WAR DIARY
or
INTELLIGENCE SUMMARY
(Erase heading not required.)

Instructions regarding War Diaries and Intelligence
Summaries are contained in F. S. Regs., Part II.
and the Staff Manual respectively. Title Pages
will be prepared in manuscript.

Place	Date	Hour	Summary of Events and Information	Remarks and references to Appendices
HOCQUINCOURT	22.7.16		All sections resting	
	23.7.16		Coy left HOCQUINCOURT 2pm, marched to PONT REMY Sta. Time of entraining 2¾ hrs. Train departed 11.58 pm.	
	24.7.16		Train arrived ST OMER 7am. Time of detraining 1½ hrs. Marched to STAPLE arriving 2pm.	
STAPLE	25.7.16 to 27.7.16		Coy Training in morning	
	28.7.16	10 am	Coy marched via CAESTRE and METEREN to billets on road ½ mile S.W. of ST JAN CAPPEL arriving 12.30 pm.	
ST JAN CAPPEL	29.7.16 to 31.7.16		Coy training	
do.	1.8.16	10.15 am	Inspection of Coy in marching order by Gen. Morse, Comg. 18th Division. Capt. Tyler in command of Coy. (DR G.H.Q. 16 A/15380 of 20.7.16)	
			Casualties during month	
	1.7.16 to 31.7.16		1 Officer killed 13.7.16 1 Officer wounded 1.7.16	
			6 O.R. killed 26 O.R. wounded 2 O.R. sent to base medically unfit (certified by D.G.M.S.)	
			1 NCO injured from kopjetest (remained with Co.)	
			1 Officer joined from base 5.7.16. 1 Officer joined proceeded 17.7.16 (reinforcements)	
			37 O.R. joined from base (reinforcements)	
			2 riding horses evacuated to NOMS.	

Ashcum Rtho.
Lieut 92nd Field Co R.E.

2449 Wt. W14957/M90 750,000 1/16 J.B.C. & A. Forms/C.2118/12.

Army Form C. 2118.

WAR DIARY
or
INTELLIGENCE SUMMARY
(Erase heading not required.)

AUG 1916. 92nd Field Co. R.E.   Vol. XIII

Sheet 1.

Place	Date	Hour	Summary of Events and Information	Remarks and references to Appendices
ST JAN CAPPEL	1/8/16	10.15am	Inspection of Coy on marching order by Gen Monro Comg 118th Div. Capt Tyler confirmed in command of Coy. (P/G GHQ No A/15380 of 20.7.16)	
"	2/8/16 to 3/8/16		Coy Training	
"	4/8/16	5 pm	Coy marched to ERQUINGHEM arriving 9.30pm. Sappers 1 no 1, 3 & 4 Sections in huts at ERIS POT, remainder of Coy in huts at ERQUINGHEM. Taking over from	
"	5/8/16		Coy of R.N.Z.E. Trenches 48 to 57.	
			No. 1 Section. Built new H.Q. for Left Coy of Left Battn. in front line. Built new H.Q. for Right Coy of Left Battn. in support line. Built bombproof for Battn. H.Q. in subsidiary line. Rebuilt dellies in subsidiary line.	
	6/8/16 to 14/8/16		No. 3 Section. Dismantled and removed old pumping plant at Brewery for further water supply, replacing with trenchplant complete (Merriweather Steam pump). Repairing and sandbagging Battn. H.Q. under bridge at CULVERT FARM. Dismantling	
BOIS GRENIER	"		and sandbagging Battn HQ. Reduced Dispatch Room, field Messing, S.A.A. and other cellars. Water billets in the village.	
			No. 2 Section. Built emergency Battn HQ under bridge at JOCKS JOY. Built dugouts, 5 more at JOCKS JOY. Making instructional wire entanglements for Battn notice boards, portainers, loopholes. Running carpenters shop.	
CULVERT FARM	"			
JOCKS JOY	"			
ERQUINGHEM	"			

Army Form C. 2118.

WAR DIARY
or
INTELLIGENCE SUMMARY

(Erase heading not required.)

92nd Field Coy RE.   Sheet 2.

Place	Date	Hour	Summary of Events and Information	Remarks and references to Appendices
BOIS GRENIER	15/8/16 to 21/8/16		Propping cellars, making air shafts and bursters ontop and sandbagging round sides of houses. Running water supply at Brewery and fitting permanent pipes.	
"JOCKS JOY"	"		Completed 5 new dugouts.	
"SHAFTESBURY AV:"	"		Revetting sides with frames – night work.	
"BIRDCAGE"	"		Propping cellars.	
"B.G." lines	"		Completed C.O.'s bombproof dugout at Battn. H.Q. Constructed signallers dugout. Three other small bomb proof	
Trench 51-58	"		Strengthened front line at junction with Left Brigade and fire step revetted in places	
Tramway Avenue	"		Sides revetted and tramway repaired whereneeded.	
	22/8/16		Handed over to 207th Field Co R.E., an officer being shown all work in progress & proposed.	
	"	4 pm	Coy. marched from ERQUINGHEM to ESTAIRES arriving 7pm.	
ESTAIRES	23/8/16 24/8/16		Drill and route marching.	
	25/8/16	9.45am 5.05pm	Marched from ESTAIRES to MERVILLE, arriving 11.30 am. Entrained in 1½ hrs. Train departed 3 pm. Train arrived BRYAS. Detrained in 1 hr. Marched to ROCOURT, arriving 8pm.	
ROCOURT	26/8/16 to 31/8/16		Coy training. Casualties during month.	
	1/9/16 to 31/8/16		1 O.R. evacuated to C.C.S. 1 Light Draft Horse and 2 Riding Horses evacuated to M.V.S. 1 Light Draft Horse died. Pthuria X70.5. 9 O.R. joined the Company from Base (Reinforcements). for O.C. 92nd Field Coy RE	

2449 Wt. W4957/M90 759,000 1/16 J.B.C.& A¹ Forms/C.2118/12.

Army Form C. 2118.

WAR DIARY
or
INTELLIGENCE SUMMARY
(Erase heading not required.)

Vol 14
92nd Field Co. R.E. Sheet I

Place	Date	Hour	Summary of Events and Information	Remarks and references to Appendices
ROCOURT	1-9-16 to 7-9-16	—	Coy training on MORCHY-BRETON training area. Repairing and maintaining rifle range at ROCOURT	
	8-9-16	—	Demonstration to 55th Inf Bde of intensive digging, and various forms of strong points	
	9-9-16	10 am	Coy marched from ROCOURT to CANETTEMONT arriving 4.15 pm	
	10-9-16	10 am	Coy marched from CANETTEMONT to BREVILLERS arriving 1 pm	
	11-9-16	6.30 am	Coy marched from BREVILLERS to PUCHEVILLERS arriving 4.30 pm	
			N.B. No men fell out during this three days march, but a great deal of fatigue was imposed on the men owing to the 55th Bde who marched behind the field by behind "B" Echelon transport in which march discipline was very bad.	
PUCHEVILLERS	12-9-16 to 17-9-16		Coy training. Senior N.C.O. visited No 7 R.E. Park to see Inglis bridge	
	18-9-16	9 am	Coy marched from PUCHEVILLERS to ACHEUX arriving 11.45 am	
ACHEUX STN.	19-9-16 to 21-9-16		No. 1 Section laid trestles of three huts for rest camps. Two 34'×22' and one 68'×22'. Built framework and roof of one of the 34' huts.	
VARENNES Timber Prep.	22-9-16 to 24-9-16		No. 1 Section built framework of 76'×25' hut. Made 7 heavy trestles for bridge at BROOKERS GAP with cross bracings for joining up trestles	
ACHEUX STN.	19-9-16 to 24-9-16		No. 2 Section made framework and roof of one 34' hut.	
ACHEUX	..		Repair & billets. Built 55 beds. Built group latrine. Made 4 heavy beds for 60 pr. T.M. Battery. Hole for tin discs with Ammonia nitrate for dueling rifle attack.	

Army Form C. 2118.

WAR DIARY
or
INTELLIGENCE SUMMARY
(Erase heading not required.)

Instructions regarding War Diaries and Intelligence Summaries are contained in F. S. Regs., Part II. and the Staff Manual respectively. Title Pages will be prepared in manuscript.

Sheet 2.

Place	Date	Hour	Summary of Events and Information	Remarks and references to Appendices
ACHEUX	19-9-16 to 24-9-16		No. 3 Section rebuilt hut for Bd' Sec School; rebuilt 3 huts for Sanitary Section; repaired roof of Divl. Stores. Lined CRE's office with matchboarding. Making 70 direction boards for Timber. 36 division boards for wounded. Latrines for Divl. HQ. General repairs to Divl. HQ.	
"	"		No.1 Section made 193 beds in various billets – strongpoints in two or three tier bunklers at Will "E" repaired.	
VIGNACOURT Timber park	25-9-16 to 29-9-16		No.1 Section completed workshops 78'x28'. Constructed 2 platforms for saw benches 42'x12'.	
ACHEUX	"		Made 6 heavy trestles for bridge at CROOKERS GAP. Laid stop piping & fittings for water troughs	
" STA	"		No.2 Section completed two 34'x22' huts except for internal fittings	
ACHEUX	"		Constructed 209 beds in selected billets. Repaired Wells F and G	
			Reconnaissance made of all billets trestles. Report troops sent to CRE.	
	30-9-16	10 a.m.	Coy marched to MARTINSART relieving 105 Fd Co RE. Horse transport left at HEDAUVILLE.	
			Casualties	
Recount	2-9-16		Two N.C.O.'s joined company from base.	
"	8-9-16		1 Light Draft Horse arrived.	
"	9-9-16		Left at Recount Sick	
Puchvillers	14-9-16		Lieut Hughes R.E. left to assume 2nd in Command of 79th Field Coy RE.	
"	16-9-16		Driver Pugh transferred to 79th Field Coy RE.	
"	14-9-16		1 Lieut Dhynt R.E. joined from Base.	
Acheux	20-9-16		1 2/D Hafferield joined 135th Army Troops Coy RE.	
"	23-9-16		1 Lieut Finch joined 135th Army Troops Coy RE.	
"	27-9-16		1 N.C.O. hand'd over 76 Men 2 Bd'ts to fall under for manoeuvres	
"	28-9-16		Two Light Draft Horses arrived	
"	28-9-16		1 Driver joined the Company from 105 Field Coy RE.	

Richmond Lieut 92nd Field Coy

No OC. 92nd Field Coy RE.

WAR DIARY
INTELLIGENCE SUMMARY
(Erase heading not required.)

Army Form C. 2118.

Vol 15

92nd Field Co. R.E.

Sheet 1.

Place	Date	Hour	Summary of Events and Information	Remarks and references to Appendices
	1-10-16 to 4-10-16		Water supplies taken over from 105th Field Co RE as follows – Two pumping plants in MARTINSART, one in THIEPVAL WOOD, one at CRUCIFIX CORNER. The plant at THIEPVAL WOOD was frequently shelled, and when all their supplies were handed over to 80th Field Co RE on 4-10-16, pumping at that point was discontinued. The other supplies and pipe lines were run and patrolled satisfactorily, except one in MARTINSART, which the petrol engine was not always running. Another engine, run little larger, was fixed by R.T. Co. and failed to carry out its duty.	
LANCASHIRE DUMP	1-10-16 to 2-10-16		One section building splinter proof huts for fatigue parties working on the railway. Work taken over from 105th Field Co. & handed over to 80th Field Co.	
SCHWABEN REDOUBT	3-10-16		One section took over from 80th Field Co. Infantry party failed to report. There not being any materials no work was accomplished.	
"	4-10-16		O.C. and Nos 1,3 & 4 Sections moved up into dugouts near the redoubt.	
"	5-10-16		Attack by Infantry on remainder objectives. Points allotted for the RE to consolidate were not captured to 0.C. ordered 3rd Section back to MARTINSART at 12.5 pm. No 1 Sect carried water to German dugout to final to MARTINSART in evening.	
	6-10-16	9 am	Coy marched to HEDAUVILLE. Mr Thomas to huts for the night.	
	7-10-16	7 am	Transport marched to AUTHEUX via ACHEUX, SARTON, DOULLENS & HEM arriving 5 pm.	
		9 am	Sappers marched to ACHEUX Sta. to train similar rate 4 pm. Men obtained 3 cattle trucks &

Army Form C. 2118.

WAR DIARY
or
INTELLIGENCE SUMMARY
(Erase heading not required.)

92nd Field Coy RE   Sheet 2.

Instructions regarding War Diaries and Intelligence Summaries are contained in F. S. Regs., Part II. and the Staff Manual respectively. Title Pages will be prepared in manuscript.

Place	Date	Hour	Summary of Events and Information	Remarks and references to Appendices
	8-10-16		Sworn Pioneer train. Detrained at CANDAS Stn. 3am. Arrived AUTHEUX 4.30 am.	
	10-10-16	9 am	Coy. less 2 Sections marched to HEM. No.2 Section detached for work at FIENVILLERS, has section detached for work at CANDAS.	
HEM	11-10-16		Two Sections repairing billets	
	15-10-16		One Section repairing billets. Rejoined Coy at HEM on 15-10-16	
CANDAS	"		One Section repairing billets erecting huts etc. Rejoined Coy at HEM on 15-10-16	
FIENVILLERS				
	16.10.16	11.30 am	Coy marched from HEM to HERISSART arriving 6 pm	
	17.10.16	8.45 am	Coy marched from HERISSART to bivouac ½ mile NW of ALBERT, arriving 3.30 pm	
	18.10.16	2.30 pm	Coy marched from bivouac to USNA REDOUBT, 1 mile NE of ALBERT	
USNA REDOUBT	19.10.16		Cleaning out & repairing dugouts for habitation. Section Officers & N.C.O.s made tour of new sector – HESSIAN TRENCH neighbourhood.	
TARA HILL	19.10.16		No.3 Section commenced work on new Divl HQ at TARA HILL. Reinforced by No.4 Section on	
	23.10.16		20.10.16. Divl HQs. completed on 23rd, including HQs for 11th and 25th Bat RA.	
USNA REDOUBT	"		Nos 1 & 2 Sections clearing dugouts & repairing accommodation. Also reconnoited forward area tramways tramway not parallel forming up trenches, with intentions of commn lines trenches in squares R22 b,c,d & d of trench map 57D SE. Supervised digging of same.	
HESSIAN TRENCH	21.10.16			
	24.10.16			
ALBERT	22.10.16	2.30 pm	Dismounted of Coy marched to ALBERT from USNA, billets in RUE D'AMELY. Horselines remained at USNA.	
	22.10.16		No.3 Section cleaning billets which were occupied daily, repairing flooring. Also made notice boards	
	29.10.16			

Army Form C. 2118.

WAR DIARY
or
INTELLIGENCE SUMMARY
(Erase heading not required.)

Instructions regarding War Diaries and Intelligence Summaries are contained in F. S. Regs., Part II. and the Staff Manual respectively. Title Pages will be prepared in manuscript.

92nd Field Co RE

Place	Date	Hour	Summary of Events and Information	Remarks and references to Appendices
	23.10.16		Fatigue parties provided Enlistment Hornthin parties for transport of RE material to Coy and Nos 1 and 2 Sections marched to Brigade Sector (this in dugouts 0E of the sector at MOUQUET FARM. Evacuation at junction of HESSIAN and RIFLE TRENCHES.	Sheet 3
R.12,27,28,33,30 Trench map 57DSE	24.10.16 to 31.10.16		Nos 1 and 2 Sections repairing dugouts in Brigade Sector, clearing and getting tunnels, making advanced prisoners cage; building steel shelters for wounded, making trestles tracks for the track from MOUQUET FARM to RIFLE TRENCH; building splinterproof cover for cookhouses. Plan made of dugouts in Old Sector. Shopkeeping up of damaged dugouts preparing enhanced increased the accommodation in that Sector by 50%. Rations for this sectors flight RE stores taken nightly to MOUQUET by pack horse	
X14 b 3.9	30.10.16		with a working party of 720 men commenced clearing site for large camps of NISSEN Bow HUTS. Also transported huts from ATELEUX to the site. This work stopped on Oct 31st owing to change of Corps boundaries.	
KAY DUMP Q34 e 2.1	22.10.16 29.10.16 to 31.10.16		Sections installed for taking charge of arriving RE materials. Later these by parties of 10 AforCn from POZIERES ROAD dump at X 9 b curled ?, under daily supervision of 15 NE Section.	
ALBERT	30.10.16		Began making hot food boxes for RE.	

2449 Wt. W14957/M90 750,000 1/16 J.B.C. & A. Forms/C.2118/12.

Army Form C. 2118.

WAR DIARY
or
INTELLIGENCE SUMMARY
(Erase heading not required.)

92nd Field Coy RE

SHEET 4

Place	Date	Hour	Summary of Events and Information	Remarks and references to Appendices
			Casualties during month of October 1916	
Martinsart	2-10-16		1 O.R. evacuated to O.C. Wagon Depot R.O.D.	
"	2-10-16		1 Officer arrived from base as reinforcement	
"	2-10-16		2 Light Draft Horses evacuated to M.V.S.	
"	2-10-16		1 Sergt reported missing from 26-9-16	
"	4-10-16		1 Light Draft Horse evacuated to M.V.S.	
	5-10-16		1 O.R. killed in action	
Authuile	8-10-16		1 O.R. evacuated to Hospital	
HEM	10-10-16		1 Light Draft Horse evacuated to M.V.S.	
"	13-10-16		1 Light Draft Horse evacuated to M.V.S	
"	16-10-16		3 Light Draft Horses arrived	
"	15-10-16		1 Light Draft Horse evacuated to M.V.S	
Una Redout	22-10-16		1 OR on leave for work on Munitions	
Albert	25-10-16		2 O.R. arrived from base as reinforcements	

Ashurst Lieut R.E.
for O.C. 92nd Field Coy RE

Army Form C. 2118.

WAR DIARY
or
INTELLIGENCE SUMMARY
(Erase heading not required.)

92nd Field Co. RE Sheet I 9 of 16

Place	Date	Hour	Summary of Events and Information	Remarks and references to Appendices
MOUQUET FARM	1-11-16 to 10-11-16		O.C. Company and Nos 1 and 2 Sections lived in dugouts, the following work was carried out:–	
do.			Cleared and repaired entrance to dugouts of 55th Inf. Bde H.Q.	
STUFF REDOUBT			Took over O.P. under construction by 79th Field Co. R.E. and finished	
MOUQUET FARM			Constructed system of drainage for extensions	
			Maintenance of roads/duckwalk from TULLOCH CORNER to MOUQUET FARM.	
			Made and erected direction boards at trench junctions, and boundary boards for circuits, showing positions taken up by all units.	
			Maintenance of LANCASHIRE TRENCH	
			Drained sunken roads at MOUQUET FARM.	
			Maintenance of water supply to-sects	
			Making small shelters for section in front line	
			Extension of dugout at R.28.d.56., and clearing & opening out with necessary repairs about 12 other dugouts	
			Making mining frames and organising the construction of 16 dugouts by infantry. Running dumps at POZIERES and getting all R.E. materials forward to section by tramline.	
X 13 b 28	1-11-16 to 10-11-16		No. 3 and No. 4 Sections erecting NISSEN BOW HUTS – number completed = 31. } No. 3 & 4 Sections living in ALBERT.	
			Also made Hutments, 11 special hut feet contained for Division.	
			Nos. 3 and 4 Sections returned Nos. 1 and 2 Sections. O.C. remained at MOUQUET FARM living with Rifle H.Q., 55th	
	10-11-16		Nos. 3 and 4 Sections carried out work as follows:-	
	11-11-16 to 23-11-16		Clearing, draining & maintaining LANCASHIRE TRENCH	
			Making mining frames and organising construction of dugouts by infantry	
			Repairing water supply to sects.	

2449 Wt. W14957/M90 750,000 1/16 J.B.C. & A. Forms/C.2118/12.

WAR DIARY or INTELLIGENCE SUMMARY

Army Form C. 2118.

92nd Field Co. RE   Sheet II

Place	Date	Hour	Summary of Events and Information	Remarks and references to Appendices
MOUQUET FARM	11.11.16 to 23.11.16		Repairing gd walk TULLOCH CORNER — MOUQUET FARM. Running dumps at POZIERES, TULLOCH CORNER, and RIFLE TRENCH & getting RE materials forward	
FABECK			Cleaning & maintaining FABECK TRENCH	
ZOLLERN REDOUBT			Opening out and repairing 5 dugouts in the ZOLLERN REDOUBT	
FIELD TRENCH			Cleaning & deepening FIELD TRENCH	
DESIRE TRENCH			Strong point made at R.16.c.66 in newly captured line.	
			Gd walk carried forward from MOUQUET FARM to FIELD TRENCH, along FIELD TRENCH to REGINA	
			Mule track laid out with luminous flags in anticipation of advance.	
			Plan & report made of all dugouts in REGINA, HESSIAN, MOUQUET FARM, ZOLLERN REDOUBT	
			New tramway in line of FIELD TRENCH between REGINA & HESSIAN.	
			Handing over all work to 3rd Fld Co of 61st Div.	
			Subbing HESSIAN TRENCH east of FIELD TRENCH	
			Maintenance work in FIELD TRENCH	
			Made dugouts for I section RE in gravel pit near MOUQUET FARM	
			Put in REGINA TRENCH	
			Clearing at ZOLLERN REDOUBT	
			Making culvert at TULLOCH CORNER	
	27.11.16		heavy gd walk MOUQUET FARM to THIEPVAL ROAD	
			No. 3 & 4 Sections returned to billets in ALBERT	
X.13.b.28	11.11.16 to 22.11.16		Nos. 1 & 2 Sections erecting NISSEN Bow HUTS — Total completed = 80 (including 31 by Nos. 3 & 4 Sects 1st–10th) Also made latrines for officers and men, and cookhouse.	

Army Form C. 2118.

WAR DIARY
or
INTELLIGENCE SUMMARY

(Erase heading not required.)

92nd FIELD CO. R.E.   Sheet III

Instructions regarding War Diaries and Intelligence Summaries are contained in F. S. Regs., Part II. and the Staff Manual respectively. Title Pages will be prepared in manuscript.

Place	Date	Hour	Summary of Events and Information	Remarks and references to Appendices
X.ID.10	23-11-16		No 1 & 2 Sections collected all spare materials from camp at X.13.b.2.5. and transported to tunnels in NAB VALLEY at X.1.D.1.D.	
	24-11-16 to 27-11-16		No 1 & 2 Section making NISSEN BOW HUTS. 3 completed - 12 others under construction.	
	28-11-16		Coy packed up ready for moving on 29th (now cancelled in turn)	
	29-11-16		Improvements to billets & trenchlines	
	30-11-16		Reconnaissance of new work on YELLOW LINE north of COURCELETTE. Coy had baths.	
			Casualties during Month	
Mouquet Farm	8-10-16		1 O.R. Wounded & evacuated	
	10-11-16		1 O.R. evacuated to C.C.S.	
	9-11-16		1 O.R. Wounded & evacuated	
	20-11-16		2 O.R. joined from base as reinforcements	
	13-11-16		5 L.D. (?) re-examined as reinforcements	
	15-11-16		2 L.D. Horses evacuated to M.V.S	
	13-11-16		2 O.R. transferred to 118th Railway Company	

Brown Capt RE
O.C. 92nd Field Coy RE

WAR DIARY
or
INTELLIGENCE SUMMARY
(Erase heading not required.)

Army Form C. 2118

92 Fd Coy R.E.
December 1916.
Vol 17

Place	Date	Hour	Summary of Events and Information	Remarks and references to Appendices
ALBERT OVILLERS	1-12-16		Company moved to near OVILLERS-LA-BOISELLE.	
"	2-12-16		Work on Billets	
"	3-12-16		Work on Billets	
"	4 "		Work on Yellow line. Dug outs, wiring, transports. 1 OR transferred to 56 Fd Army Coy. 3 OR joined from Base.	
"	5 "		"	
"	6 "		"	
"	7 "		"	
"	8 "		" 2 reinforcements	
"	9 "		" 1 reinforcement	
"	10 "		" 1 OR killed	
"	11 "		" 1 OR evacuated	
"	12 "		"	
"	13 "		"	
"	14 "		"	
"	15 "		"	
"	16 "		" 2 LDH rec'd	
"	17 "		"	
"	18 "		"	
"	19 "		"	
"	20 "		" Packing Company transports.	
"	21 "		Transport moved to NOUVION-EN-PONTHIEU by road. 1 OR transferred to Newark.	
NOUVION-EN-PON THIEU	22 "		Company less transport moved to NOUVION-EN-PONTHIEU by rail.	
"	23 "		Work on Billets &c. 1 man to Hospital. 1 horse evacuated.	
"	24 "		"	
"	25 "		Day off Billets.	
"	26 "		Work on Billets.	
"	27 "		Work on 63rd Div. & School - for Artillery - Incinerators - Cattle troughs - Recreation rooms &c. 2 LDH evacuated	
"	28 "		"	
"	29 "		Work on 63rd Div School. Construction of latrines, sheds, huts, ovens, incinerating stabling, horse standings, harbour sheds, 2 LD Hamanites	
"	30 "		" Erection of Nissen huts, Builders Bath House. Construction huts for S. Ambulance " 10 R joined from Base.	
"	31 "		" Construction of kitchen waste troughs " " "	

M Wagner Capt RE
OC No 92nd (Fd) Coy RE

Army Form C. 2118

Vol 18

92 Field Co. RE.

WAR DIARY
or
INTELLIGENCE SUMMARY
(Erase heading not required.)

JANUARY 1917

Instructions regarding War Diaries and Intelligence Summaries are contained in F.S. Regs., Part II. and the Staff Manual respectively. Title Pages will be prepared in manuscript.

Place	Date	Hour	Summary of Events and Information	Remarks and references to Appendices
NOUVION-EN-PONTHIEU	1		Construction of Bath House and fitting up baths. Fitting up 63RD Bn School. Bundry Huts etc in village. Erection of stables.	
	2		" " and fitting up drying room	
	3		" "	and Nissen Bow Huts. Due OR eventuals to Mc Cauch (Gen Hosp)
	4		" "	Fitting up hospital of 3RD F.A. Construction of Bridge
	5		Completing Bridge over Avion. Continuation of Bn Baths in REnomé. Fitting up 63RD Bn Huts of Bathing of fields and also at NOLETTES. Construction of RE stores, hops + Beng. pits for Bath House. Erection of Bath House for 3RD F.A. Erection of Nissen Bowhuts and stables in village. Construction of Rue Bowhut.	
	6		Huts, woods and Bath House. NOUVION. Building of Field Hospital 3.F.A. and erection of Nissen Bow Huts. Erection of hut for 63rd Bn School. Construction of stables. Contg. Y.M.C.A. hut NOUVION. Bucking of fields at NOLETTES. Erection of Nissen Bow Huts for 2 L.D. now used as Reinforcement	
	7		Continuation of work on hospital for 3 Field Ambulance. Erection of Nissen hut at 63rd Bn School. Erection of Nissen Hut	
	8		Work at Field Ambulance hospital. Construction of stable/latrine. Erection of Nissen hut. Bathhouse in RE wood x2	Fitting up on Y.M.C.A. Hut
	9		Finishing off Bath House. Construction of Nissen Bow Huts at Bn School	
	10		Company left NOUVION-EN-PONTHIEU for LE PLESSIEL. Arrived at LE PLESSIEL 1:0 pm and used its billets.	
	11		" LE PLESSIEL for COULONVILLERS arriving at 5:0 pm used its billets	
	12		" COULONVILLERS for OUTREBOIS arrived at 2:0 pm used its billets	
OUTREBOIS	13		Inspection of Company. Instruction in use of Box Respirators.	
	14		Company left OUTREBOIS for BERUQUESNE arriving at 4:30 pm used its billets 2:00 to	
BERUQUESNE	15		Cleaning and repair of Company transport and equipment.	
	16		Company left BERUQUESNE for MIDLAND HUTS W.9.b.9.5. taking over from 1/3 South Midland RE work of company in reserve	
MIDLAND HUTS W9.b9.5	17		Work on Divisional Head Quarters. Construction of Nissen Bow Huts Stables. Work in camp. Construction of paths. Cleaning of huts. Construction of frames, hurdles, pickets.	
	18		Continuation of work at Div H.Q. Linking of wells at camp Re Cover. Repair of huts and dugouts for 54 F.A. Construction of frames for road repair. Work at RE dump. Repair to hutments in camp.	

WAR DIARY
or
INTELLIGENCE SUMMARY
(Erase heading not required.)

Army Form C. 2118

Instructions regarding War Diaries and Intelligence Summaries are contained in F.S. Regs., Part II. and the Staff Manual respectively. Title Pages will be prepared in manuscript.

Place	Date	Hour	Summary of Events and Information	Remarks and references to Appendices
W9 C 9.5	19-1-17		Burying Midland Huts. Sinking Well at Crucifix Corner. Ouderdom Dump. Drawing Saw + Carpenters. Ouderdom Wood. Making Hurdles + facines. Transporting Hurdles from Wood to Dump.	Sheet 2
"	20-1-17		Flooring Huts at Montinsart. Ouderdom Dump. Drawing Saw + Carpenters Wood. Making fascines + Hurdles. Improving road to Havre line. Transporting Hurdles & fascines to Dump.	
N. of Busseboom W3 G17 Ouderdom ATN Dump W11 D82 W11 D57 W10 C18 W9 C95	21-1-17		Improvements to D H Q Repairs + improvements to Huts occupied by 10th Bn Essex Regt. Cutting brushwood & making fascines. Running Dump. Sinking Well Crucifix Corner. Supervising erection of Nissen Huts & repairing Tunnel. Making furniture etc. for permanent working parties. Painting Huts	
N of Brandhoek	22-1-17		Improvements to D H Q	

Army Form C. 2118

WAR DIARY
or
INTELLIGENCE SUMMARY
(Erase heading not required.)

Instructions regarding War Diaries and Intelligence Summaries are contained in F. S. Regs., Part II. and the Staff Manual respectively. Title Pages will be prepared in manuscript.

Place	Date	Hour	Summary of Events and Information	Remarks and references to Appendices
W3 C 17 Aveluy Wood A T N Dump W11 D 8 2 W11 D 5 7 W10 C 18 W 9 b 9 5	22-1-17		Repairs & improvements to huts occupied by 10th Bn Essex Regt. Sheet 3. 1 Section R.E. Butting Breastwork & making fascines. 1 Section R.E. 1/3 Platoons Infantry Running Dump. Finishing well at Buirfex Corner. Supervising erection of Nissen Huts & repairing Tunnel. } 1 Section R.E. Doing making furniture for permanent working parties. } 4 Platoons Infantry Painting Huts.	
N of Bouzincourt W 3 C 17 Aveluy Wood A T N Dump W11 D 8 2 W11 D 5 7 W 10 C 18 W 9 b 9 5	23-1-17		Improvements to D.H.Q. — 1 Section R.E. Repairs & improvements to huts occupied by 10th Bn Essex Regt. 1 Section R.E. Butting Breastwork & making fascines. 1 Section R.E. and 3 Platoons Infantry Running Dump. Sinking Well at Buirfex Corner — Completed today — Depth 20'6". } 1 Section R.E. Supervising erection of Nissen Huts. Repairing Tunnel. } 4 Platoons Infantry making furniture for permanent working parties. Painting Huts.	
	24-1-17		At work as on 23rd — except well at Buirfex Corner — finished Tradition. 50 Carpenters permanently detailed from Infantry for work in Dump making wheelbarrows etc.	
A T N Dump	25-1-17		At work as on 24th. Also opened huts at MARTINSART for 53rd Adv.. 1 N.C.O & 12 men sent to 55th Sub. Bde at HEDAUVILLE to erect extra huts to European huts	

r875 Wt. W593/826 1,000,000 4/15 J.B.C. & A. A.D.S.S./Forms/C. 2118.

WAR DIARY
or
INTELLIGENCE SUMMARY

(Erase heading not required.)

Army Form C. 2118

Place	Date	Hour	Summary of Events and Information	Remarks and references to Appendices
DIV. HQrs.	26.1.17		1 Section R.E. at Divl. HQrs. improving accommodation	Sheet No.
MARTINSART	"		1 " at MARTINSART WOOD do.	
PIERWOOD	28.1.17		1 " in PIERWOOD making brushwood fascines, hurdles	
			3 Platoons }	
AVELUY SIDINGS			1 Section R.E.} Running Divl. Dumps, canteens, workshops. Providing men also for 35th Bde. at	
			4 Platoons } HEDAUVILLE to erect Nissen huts to. Dismantled road to Divl. School at HEDAUVILLE on	
			Nissen Hut. Supervising erection of huts. Reconstructing dugouts by 57th Field Ambulance	
			at W.11.d.59. Painting huts west of river Ancre. Camp improvements &c.	
	29.1.17		1 Section R.E. at Divl. HQrs. improving accommodation	
	"		1 " at MARTINSART WOOD do.	
	"		1 " erecting Nissen huts at WARWICK CAMP MARSROAD. Assisted in moving by 3 platoons	
			of 29th. In afternoon also 3 platoons were transferred for work with the Tunnelling Co. R.E.	
			carpentry	
	30.1.17		1 " Running Divl. Dumps, canteens, workshops. Arrived by 4 platoons.	
			Also 6 sappers at 65th Inf.Bde. HEDAUVILLE erecting bidets, and repairing baths.	
			3 sappers at 18th Divl. School. 3 sappers erecting 54th Field Ambulance. 1 sapper R.E. carpentry	
			painting huts west of river ANCRE	
			Casualties during month	6 O.R. evacuated sick
				5 L.D. knee wounded
				3 L.D. knee arrived
			Lt. W. Pitman R.E. joined from Base 16.1.17	
			Lt. Hudson R.E. transferred to Heavy Branch M.G. Corps 19.1.17	
			Capt. Tyler R.E. do 17th Corps 19.1.17	
			Major Rosm. Hayman D.S.O. R.E. award Gremuard Coy. 26.1.17	
			Major Hayman to RE School of Instruction 31.1.17	

R.A. Nunn
Capt. R.E.
O.C. 92nd Field Coy R.E.

1875 Wt. W593/826 1,000,000 4/15 J.B.C. & A. A.D.S.S./Forms/C. 2118.

Army Form C. 2118

WAR DIARY
or
INTELLIGENCE SUMMARY

92nd Field Co. R.E.

Sheet I

(Erase heading not required.)

Instructions regarding War Diaries and Intelligence Summaries are contained in F.S. Regs., Part II. and the Staff Manual respectively. Title Pages will be prepared in manuscript.

February 1917

Place	Date	Hour	Summary of Events and Information	Remarks and references to Appendices
X2C4.3	1-2-17	1 pm	1 Section marched to Angeles in test German frontline, for work in ZOLLERN TRENCH	
MARTINSARTWOOD	"		1 Section improving accommodation of huts – infantry parties arrived with battalion living there.	
W12 D59	"		" erecting Corps minor aviation hut – with 12 infantry	
W9 D99	"		" dismantling Corps minor aviation hut near DUMP trenching near MACKENZIE HUTS at W9 D99 with 12 infantry	
W12 D93	"		" erecting Church Army hut with 20 infantry	
HEDAUVILLE	"		" erecting beds and repairing baths for 55th Inf. Bde.	
W7B	"		1 Section improving accommodation at Divl. HQrs.	
W4M	"		1 Section arrived by 4 platoons infantry 45D } Running Divl. RE dump, construct workshops, etc. Also 3 sappers at 11th Divl. School. infantry Gradmen	
R26 D39	2-2-17 to 3-2-17		Work as per 1-2-17. Completion takes work in dugout in ZOLLERN TRENCH under 3 kilos end	
			12 infantry on east shift transit	
VII A96			Two sappers sent to D.A.C. to supervise erection of 7.6 nun power driven chaff cutter.	
Divl HQ	4-2-17		Improvements to billets (1 Section)	
W3 C17	"		Repairs improvements & huts & Support Bde. (1 Section)	
R28 D38	"		Repairing / repairing elephant mens 3 shifts – (1 Section & 3 platoons)	
W11 C30	"		Running dump, sandwork workshops – (1 Section & platoon, 20 infantry Gradmen)	
FORCEVILLE	"		Erecting dugout shed (2 sappers)	
HEDAUVILLE	"		Billet improvements for various Brigade (5 sappers)	
VII 54	"		Erecting forms Chipfoulh (4 sappers)	
W9 D97	"		Erecting aviation hut (Nissen 60x20) – (4 sappers 12 infantry)	
W12 D76	"		Erecting aviation hut – Nissen 60x20 (3 sappers 20 infantry)	
MARTINSART	"		Erecting baths (2 sappers). Repairing Billets HQ 5 Corps.	
VARENNES	"		Repairing Billets HQ 5 Corps (2 sappers)	

Army Form C. 2118

WAR DIARY
or
INTELLIGENCE SUMMARY
(Erase heading not required.)

92nd Field Co R.E. Sheet-2

Place	Date	Hour	Summary of Events and Information	Remarks and references to Appendices
			February 1917	
Bn. HQ	5th		Improving accommodation (1 Section)	
R25 b38	"		Extending dugout messes (1 Section & 3 platoons in 3 shifts)	
W11 c 30	"		Running dump, sandbank, workshop etc. (1 Section, 3 platoons & 50 infantry tradesmen)	
FORCEVILLE	"		Erecting dugouts for 58th F.A. (2 sappers)	
HEDAUVILLE	"		Improving billets for Cannon Bde. (5 sappers)	
V11 a 66	"		Erecting Armour Clift cmltn (4 sappers)	
N9 d 97	"		Erecting Accession hut (10 sappers, 10 infantry)	
W12 d 76	"		Erecting Accession hut (10 sappers, 10 infantry)	
MARTINSART	"		Repairing baths (2 sappers) (Repairing trails (2 sappers))	
VARENNES	"		Erecting spray baths (2 sappers)	
Div HQ	6th		Improving accommodation (1 Section)	
R 25 b38	"		Extending dugout (1 Section & 3 platoons in 3 shifts)	
W 11 c 30	"		Running dump, sandbank, workshop etc. (1 Section, 3 platoons & 50 infantry tradesmen)	
FORCEVILLE	"		Erecting Armour shed (2 sappers)	
HEDAUVILLE	"		Improving billets Cannon Bde. (5 sappers) (2 sappers) humour	
V11 d 88	"		Erecting Armour Clift cmltn (2 sappers)	
N9 d 97	"		Erecting Accession hut (10 sappers, 10 infantry)	
W12 d 76	"		Erecting Accession hut (10 sappers, 10 infantry)	
MARTINSART	"		Repairing trails (2 sappers)	
VARENNES	"		Erecting spray baths (2 sappers)	
MAILLY MAILLET	"		Collecting materials for Church Armour hut (2 sappers)	
Div HQ	7th		Improving accommodation (1 Section)	
R25 b 38	"		Extending dugout (1 Section, 3 platoons in 3 shifts)	
W11 C 30	"		Running dump, sandbank, workshop etc. (1 Section, 3 platoons & 50 infantry tradesmen)	
FORCEVILLE	"		Erecting Armour shed (2 sappers)	
HEDAUVILLE	"		Repairing billets (5 sappers)	

Army Form C. 2118

WAR DIARY
or
INTELLIGENCE SUMMARY
(Erase heading not required.)

92nd Field Coy RE

Place	Date	Hour	Summary of Events and Information	Remarks and references to Appendices
			February 1917	Sheet 3
V.11.d.88	7th		Erecting power staff cubicle (2 sappers)	
W.9.d.9	"		Erecting recreation hut (10 sappers 10 infantry)	
W.2.d.76	"		Erecting recreation hut (10 sappers 10 infantry)	
MARTINSART	"		Repairing billets (2 sappers)	
MAILLY MAILLET	"		Collecting parts of Church Army Hut (2 sappers)	
DIV. HQ	8th		Improvements to billets (1 Section)	
R.25.b.56	"		Dugout completed 23'x9' MG 15 hq 9 ZOLLERN TRENCH	
R.25.b.88	"		Commenced repairs to dugouts no. 8 ZOLLERN TRENCH } 1 Section 3 platoons	
R.22.d.61	"		Digging coop trench for water tanks	
R.32.b.9	"		Making culvert under road for water pipe	
W.11.c.30	"		Running dump southwards (6 sappers 61 infantry of 35 infantry Division)	
V.11.d.86	"		Erecting power staff cubicle (2 sappers)	
W.9.d.9	"		Erecting recreation hut (6 sappers 5 infantry)	
W.2.d.76	"		Erecting recreation hut (7 sappers 8 infantry)	
HEDAUVILLE	"		Repairing billets etc (7 sappers)	
FORCEVILLE	"		Erecting drying shed (2 sappers)	
MAILLY MAILLET	"		Collecting parts of Church Army Hut (2 sappers)	
DIV. H.Q.	9th		Improvements to billets (1 section)	
R.25.b.88	"		Repairing outstanding dugout no. 8 } 1 Section 3 platoons	
R.22.d.61	"		Digging emplacements for water tanks	
R.32.b.9	"		Making culvert under road	
W.11.c.30	"		Running dump, constructed workshops etc (6 sappers 36 infantry, 36 infantry Division)	
V.11.d.88	"		Erecting power staff cubicle (2 sappers)	
W.9.d.9	"		Erecting recreation hut (8 sappers)	

1875 Wt. W593/826 1,000,000 4/15 J.B.C. & A. A.D.S.S./Forms/C. 2118.

WAR DIARY or INTELLIGENCE SUMMARY

Army Form C. 2118

92nd Field Co. R.E. Sheet 1

Place	Date	Hour	Summary of Events and Information	Remarks and references to Appendices
W12d76	9th		Erecting recreation hut (70 sappers)	
HEDAUVILLE	"		Repairing billets & (5 sappers)	
FORCEVILLE	"		Erecting drying shed (2 sappers)	
Div H.Q.	15th		Improvements to billets (1 Section)	
R28b8x	"		Extending dugout No 8 (1 Section 3 platoons)	
R22d a1	"		Digging for water (anti-)	
R22b57	"		Making culvert under road	
W11c30	"		Running dump, sawdust, workshops etc (6 sappers 76 infantry, 36 inf tradesmen)	
V11d 55	"		Erecting power chaff cutter (2 sappers, 6 infantry)	
W9d97	"		Erecting recreation hut (8 sappers)	
W12d76	"		Erecting recreation hut (7 sappers)	
HEDAUVILLE	"		Repairs to billets (5 sappers)	
FORCEVILLE	"		Erecting drying shed (2 sappers)	
Div H.Q.	11th		Improvements to billets (1 Section)	
R28b88	"		Extending dugout No 8	
R22d41	"		Digging for water tanks (1 Section 3 platoons)	
R32b57	"		Culvert under road	
R32b95	"		Laying 4" pipes	
W11c30	"		Running dump, sawdust, workshops etc (6 sappers, 36 infantry, 36 inf tradesmen)	
Y11d 88	"		Erecting power chaff cutter (2 sappers, 6 infantry)	
W9d97	"		Erecting recreation hut (8 sappers)	
W12d76	"		Erecting recreation hut (7 sappers)	
HEDAUVILLE	"		Repairing billets etc (5 sappers)	

Army Form C. 2118

WAR DIARY
or
INTELLIGENCE SUMMARY

(Erase heading not required.)

92nd Field Coy R.E.   Sheet 5

Place	Date	Hour	Summary of Events and Information	Remarks and references to Appendices
Div. H.Q.	12th		February 1917	
			Improvements to billets (1 Section)	
R28 b36	"		Extending dugout no. 8	
R22 d41	"		Digging for water tanks } (1 Section 3 Platoons)	
R32 b87	"		Culvert for water pipes }	
R32 b94	"		Laying 4" pipes	
W11 c30	"		Running dump, armourer, workshops &c (62 sappers, 69 infantry, 36 inf tradesmen)	
Y11 d88	"		Erecting power shelter &c (2 sappers)	
N9 d97	"		Erecting recreation hut (8 sappers) completed	
W12 d76	"		Erecting recreation hut (7 sappers)	
HEDAUVILLE	"		Repairing billets &c (5 sappers)	
W9 B95	"		1 Section marched from Div H.Q. into billets at Foy Huts for work on GRANDCOURT ROAD	
ST PIERRE DIVION	13th		Repairing road left bank of river (1 Section 300 infantry)	
R29 b55	"		Extending dugout no 8	
R22 d41	"		Digging for water tanks } (1 Section 3 platoons)	
.R27 d	"		Laying 4" pipes }	
W11 c30	"		Running dump, armourer, workshops &c (62 sappers, unit 64 sappers & 34 infantry tradesmen)	
Div H.Q.	"		Making furniture (3 inf tradesmen)	
W12 d76	"		Erecting recreation hut (2 sappers) completed	
HEDAUVILLE	"		Repairing billets (5 sappers)	
X7 a L7	"		Erecting prisoners cage (10 sappers 6 infantry)	
ST PIERRE DIVION	14th		Repairing relieving road (1 section 300 infantry)	
R22 d41	"		Digging for storage tanks } (1 Section 3 platoons)	
R27 d	"		Laying 4" pipes }	

Army Form C. 2118.

WAR DIARY
or
INTELLIGENCE SUMMARY
(Erase heading not required.)

92nd Field Co R.E.   Sheet 6

Place	Date	Hour	Summary of Events and Information	Remarks and references to Appendices
W11 c 30	14th		Running dump, sawbench, workshops &c (6 sappers 56 infantry 36 inf kadramen)	
Div HQ	"		Making furniture (3 inf kadramen)	
HEDAUVILLE	"		Repairing trucks (5 sappers)	
X7 a 47	"		Erecting prisoners cage (4 sappers. 6 infantry)	
R32 b 89	"		Erecting prisoners cage (5 sappers 6 infantry)	
			The Section working on GRANDCOURT ROAD marched from W9 b 95 to dugouts at Q24 b 77	
R 13	15th		Repairing road (1 Section 180 infantry)	
R22 d 41	"		Digging for storage tanks } 1 Section 3 platoons	
R 27 d	"		Laying 4" pipes }	
W11 c 30	"		Running dump, sawbench, workshops &c (6 sappers 73 infantry, 30 inf kadramen)	
Div HQ	"		Making furniture (3 inf kadramen)	
HEDAUVILLE	"		Repairing trucks (5 sappers - withdrawn in evening)	
X7 a 47	"		Erecting Prisoners Cage (4 sappers) } completed	
R32 b 89	"		Erecting Prisoners Cage (5 sappers) }	
N12 d 24	"		Erecting Church Army hut - (2 sappers - withdrawn in evening)	
R5 d 41	"		Forming advanced R.E. dumps	
C 12	16th		Repairing road (1 Section)	
R 22 d 41	"		Storing water tanks } 1 Section 1 platoon	
R 25 a	"		Laying 4" pipes }	
R 28 a 9?	"		Branch water supply to ZOLLERN (1 Section 1 platoon)	
R 34 a	"		Work on new light railway under Canadian Ry Co.	

Army Form C. 2118.

WAR DIARY
or
INTELLIGENCE SUMMARY

(Erase heading not required.)

92nd Field Co RE.

Sheet 7

Place	Date	Hour	Summary of Events and Information	Remarks and references to Appendices
			February 1917	
W11 c 30	16th		Running dump, sawbench, workshops &c (1 Section 50 infantry 2 W tradesmen)	
R12 d 20	"		Running O.T. dump (1 cospl. 11 infantry)	
R29 c 72	"		Running RIFLE dump (1 coppl.)	
DIV H.Q.	"		Making furniture (3 int tradesmen)	
R8 A 21	"		Forming advanced RE dump	
			One permanent platoon transferred from section on water supply to dumps - 45th wo section at W9b91'	
R13	17th		Repairing GRANDCOURT ROAD (1 section)	
NAB JUNCTION to R22 d 41 R8 A 21			Forward water supply (1 section 7 platoon)	
STUFF REDOUBT			Forming advanced RE dump	
DIV HQ	"		Joking full size front (1 section 7 platoon) Making furniture (3 carps.)	
W11 c 30	"		Running dump, sawbench, workshops &c (1 Section, 60 infantry, 3 W tradesmen)	
R12 d 20	"		Running O.T. Dump (1 coppl. 11 inf.)	
R29 c 72	"		Running RIFLE Dump (1 section)	
R13	18th		Repairing GRANDCOURT ROAD (1 section)	
NAB JUNCTION to R22 d 41			Forward water supply (1 section 7 platoon)	
STUFF REDOUBT			Joking full size forward (1 section 7 platoon) Laying W net pattern	
R22 6	"			
W11 c 30	"		Running dump, sawbench, workshops &c (1 sect. 99 inf 29 tradesmen)	
R12 d 20	"		Running O.T. dump (1 cpl. 11 inf.)	
R8 C 72	"		Running RIFLE dump (1 cpl.)	
DIV HQ	"		Making furniture (3 carps)	
W 9 A 91	"		Filling out centers (div.) (5 saps)	

Army Form C. 2118.

WAR DIARY
or
INTELLIGENCE SUMMARY

(Erase heading not required.)

92" Field Co. R.E.   Sheet 8

Instructions regarding War Diaries and Intelligence Summaries are contained in F.S. Regs., Part II and the Staff Manual respectively. Title Pages will be prepared in manuscript.

Place	Date	Hour	Summary of Events and Information	Remarks and references to Appendices
	Feb 1917			
R13	19"		Repairing road (1 section)	
MR5 Junction to R22 d 44			Forward dumps supply (1 Section)	
R22b7 - R16d59			Laying tunnel tramways (1 sect + platoon) taken cards for spurs or trip	
H11 c 30	"		Running dumps a newtrack worksheops &c (1 sect + 49 inf 3rd Ed down)	
R12 A 20	"		Running O.T. dump (1 sect + 11 inf)	
R 28 C 72	"		Running RIFLE dump (1 sect)	
Div HQ	"		Making furniture (3 carps)	
R 13	20"		Repairing road (1 sect)	
R22 b 77 - R22 b 53	"		Forward work supply (1 sect + platoon)	
R22 b	"		Supply tunnel fittings (1 sect + platoon)	
	"		Cradle notation for field run	
H11 c 30	"		Running dumps a newtrack worksheops &c (1 sect + 49 inf 32 Ed down)	
R12 A 20	"		Running O.T. dump (1 sect + 11 inf)	
R 28 C 72	"		Running RIFLE dump (1 sect)	
Div HQ	"		Making furniture (3 carps)	
W9d 97	21st		Tracing up SM. Section (2 carps)	
			50" Field Co returned 92" Field Co Camps move as follows:-	
			Coy H.Q. W9 b 95 - X 2 a 14	39 tradesmen handed over to 50" Co
			1 Section Q24 b 77 - R28 e 72	7 Carlson Ponies do
			1 Section X 1 c 71 - R22 d 46	7 Troop Horses Party do
			1 Section extracted from dumps, Woodworks, etc. - X 2 a 14	
			1 Platoon X 1 c 71 - R 22 d 46	
			1 Platoon X 1 c 71 - X 2 a 14	
			1 Platoon W9 b 95 - R 28 c 72	

Army Form C. 2118.

WAR DIARY
or
INTELLIGENCE SUMMARY

92nd Field Co. R.E.   Sheet 9

(Erase heading not required.)

Instructions regarding War Diaries and Intelligence Summaries are contained in F.S. Regs., Part II and the Staff Manual respectively. Title Pages will be prepared in manuscript.

Place	Date	Hour	Summary of Events and Information	Remarks and references to Appendices
R22.d41, [6] R17.c29	22nd		Forward work supply (2 sects & platoons)	
R23.a, R22,R29a	"		Laying Wire netting (2 sects & platoons)	
W.11.c.30	"		Handing over dump	
R.12.d.20	"		do.	
D.6.H.a	"		Motor transit (2 sappers)	
R.10.d	23rd		Reply wire shoring in Boom Ravine E (West platoon) Relaying dug outs	
R.7.a	"		Sudbury tunnel (1 sect & platoon)	
R22.d41-R27.a9	"		do.	
DW HQ	"		Making furniture (2 sappers)	
P+P DUMP	"		Unloads So: Field Co. (1 NCO)	
R.17.d 20	24th.25th		Extending 2 dugouts) (1 sect & platoon)	
R22.d 88	"		do.)	
R22.d 66	"		do.) (1 sect & platoon)	
R23.c 52	"		do.)	
R2.dw-R.27.a9	"		Wire supply (2 sects & platoons)	
DW HQ	"		Making furniture (2 sappers)	
P+P DUMP	"		Carrying So: Field Co. (1 NCO)	
R22.R9, R27.c R17.b	26th.		Wire supply (2 sects & platoons)	
R17.d20	"		Extending 2 dugouts (1 out platoon)	
R5.c33	"		Relieving & platoon marched from x2.a.14 to dugouts in PETIT MIRAUMONT at R5.c.33	
P+P DUMP	"		Carrying So: Field Co. (1 NCO)	
Rd.R17.c R17.b	27th		Wire supply (2 sect & platoon)	
R5.a.15 R5.a.18	"		Mountain (West platoon)	
R5.c33	"		Other half section & platoon mounted. Clearing dugouts.	

WAR DIARY
or
INTELLIGENCE SUMMARY

Army Form C. 2118.

92nd Fuel CoRE   Shus 10.

Place	Date	Hour	Summary of Events and Information	Remarks and references to Appendices
R24 - R19 R11c	26th		hut supply (that & platoons) kinstwhs at R22 A 44 (3200 galls) was full. Extra farm house hut at R.9 C 29.	
			Pipe laid on farm BOULOGNE R11 C 53	
RSC 35			Clearing dugouts Re. (that & platoon)	
RSC 21			1 Section 1 Platoon moved from RIFLE DUMP (R28 c 72) to dugouts near PETIT INFANTRYMENT (RSC21)	
RSC 15 - RSC 18			Road clearance for artillery. (that platoon)	
			Casualties during February.	
La G.H	1st		1 OR died in Hospital (Disease)	
	7th		3 OR joined - reinforcements from Base	
	8th		1 OR transferred to No 4 General Base	
	10th		3 OR accidentally killed, 6 OR accidentally wounded.	
	16th		1 OR joined - reinforcement from Base.	
	17th		1 OR wounded slightly - remaining at duty	
	18th		1 OR wounded slightly - remaining at duty	
	19th		6 OR joined - reinforcements from Base.	
	23rd		I Lieut Boyer and 1 OR killed in action 1 OR wounded in action	
	25th		2 OR reported to Transportation Depot Boulogne	
	25th		2 LG Horses evacuated to MVS.	
	27th		1 OR killed in action - 1 OR wounded slightly, remaining with Unit.	
			Strength of Unit on Midnight 28-2-14. Officers 5 - OR Dismounted 141 OR Mounted 50 - Horses 68.	

Florence
Capt RE. 9 Fuel CoRE.
for O.C. 92

Army Form C. 2118.

18

WAR DIARY
or
INTELLIGENCE SUMMARY
(Erase heading not required.)

92nd Field Coy R.E.

Sheet 1.

Vol 20

Place	Date	Hour	Summary of Events and Information	Remarks and references to Appendices
X2a14	1st		Location of Company as follows:—	
R22d47			Coy HQ. No 2 Section with Queen's Platoon	
R5c33			No 1 Section and Tunny Platoon	
W9b95			No 3 & 4 Sections with Buffs & W.Kent Platoon	
			Horse Lines	
HESSIAN DUMP. BOIRY RAVINE			Repairing trench pathways	
R22d47			Enlarging dugout } 1 Sect + platoon	
R10b.			Repairing GRANDCOURT—MIRAUMONT RD.	
R5c			do. } 1 Sect + platoon	
R5c10-45			Repairing dugouts	
R5c33			Tankstaff 1. — Building wire traps, timber for w/w trench etc } 1 Sect/platoon (Horse lines moved to W6c03)	
			Extending dugout	
R22d41—R11c53			Tanks dugout } (1 Sect + platoon)	
K11c30	1st 2nd		Work for 50 Coy.	
L35c83.L35d33	3rd 4th 5th		Repairing road (1 Sect + platoon)	
R5c33	do		Tanks dugout } 1 Sect + platoon	
R11a78	do		Fitting Bde HQ	
R5c10-45	do		Repairing dugouts (Sect + platoon)	
R	do		Fixing notice boards at trench junctions etc	
R22d1—R11c53	do		Tanks dugout	
R11c30	do		Work for 50 Coy.	
R5c33	5th		Coy HQ moved up from X2a14	

Army Form C. 2118.

WAR DIARY
or
INTELLIGENCE SUMMARY

(Erase heading not required.)

99nd Field Co. R.E.

Part 2.

Place	Date	Hour	Summary of Events and Information	Remarks and references to Appendices
	March 1917			
R3a55_L3sd33	6th		Repairing road (1 Sect & platoon)	
R3c83	"		Water supply } (1 Sect + platoon)	
R11a75	"		Yetting Bde HQ.	
R5c10-45	"		Repairing dugouts (1 Sect + platoon)	
R3d41_R11c83	"		Water supply } 1 Sect & platoon	
R3sd53_R3sb55	"		Water supply (Pioneer Camp) }	
X7	"		Salving 2" pipes from disused main	
15111c30	"		Work for 80th Co.	
1011c30	7th-8th		Boat for 60th Co.	
L35c60-L3sd33	"		Repairing road (1 Sect & Platoon)	
R5c10-R5c45	"		Repairing & extending dugouts	
ST PIERCE DIVION	"		Salving R.E. Stores from disused dumps } 1 Sect & Platoon	
L35c9525	"		Forming forward Bde R.E. dump	
R5d18	"		do.	
R5c31_R5c66	"		Water supply } 1 Sect & platoon	
R11a75	"		Yetting at Bde HQ	
R12d41_R11c53	"		Water supply] 1 Sect & platoon - then moved from APIS VALLEY dugouts to HESSIAN TR. dugouts.	
R3sd53_R3sb55	"		Water supply }	
L35c52	9th		Construction & platoon moved into cellars (from HESSIAN TR.)	
R5c10_R5c45	"		Repairing & extending dugouts	
L35c9525	"		Forming forward Bde R.E. dump } 1 Sect & platoon	
R5d18	"		do	

Army Form C. 2118.

WAR DIARY
or
INTELLIGENCE SUMMARY
(Erase heading not required.)

92nd Turkish Co RE   Sheet 3.

Place	Date	Hour	Summary of Events and Information	Remarks and references to Appendices
RSc33_RSc83	9th		Water Supply (1 half platoon)	
R2d41_R11c83	"		Water Supply maintenance } 1 Sect platoon	
R33d93_R33b51	"		do. construction	
W11 c 30	"		Sannaiyat trenches on first dump (4)	
R2d41 - R11c53	10th		Water Supply maintenance (1 Sect platoon)	
L3sq42 - L3c07	"		Repairing road } 2 Secs & platoons	
R5d15 - R5d57	"		do	
G25 b 9015	"		Making strong point (1 Sect platoon) night work	
W11 c 30	"		H Sannaiyat trenches on 2nd dump	
R2d41_R11c53	11th		Water Supply maintenance (1 Sect platoon)	
RSc33_RSd57	"		do. construction	
RSc10_RSc45	"		Road widening	
RSc9	"		Widening at sumput openings } 1 Sect platoon	
RSc72	"		Began opening up Domino dugout	
G25 b 9015	"		Strong point attended & strengthened (1 Sect platoon) night work	
W11 c 30	"		H Sannaiyat trenches on 2nd dump	
Maasjunction_R11c53	12th		Water Supply maintenance ((1 Sect platoon)	
RSc33_RSd57	"		do. construction	
RSc10_RSc45	"		Road widenings	
RSa72	"		Dugout being opened up } do.	
W11c30	"		H Sannaiyat trenches & dumps.	
Maasjunction_R11c53	13th		Water Supply maintenance } 1 Sect platoon and 1 Coy Infantry (52)	
RSc10-RSa46	"		Road & pipe line	

WAR DIARY
INTELLIGENCE SUMMARY

(Erase heading not required.)

92nd Field Coy R.E.   Sheet 4.

Army Form C. 2118.

Place	Date	Hour	Summary of Events and Information	Remarks and references to Appendices
	March 1917			
R5c53 - R5a87	13th		Water Supply (1 sect + platoon)	
L5y145 - G31b00	"		Centrepaire	
G31b00 - G31b96	"		do.	
M1c30			do.	
NAVSTINITIAN Q4c63	14th		4 Sappers on dump	
R5a46	"		Water Supply maintenance	
L5c45 - G31b00	"		Repairing and laying own wires	} 1 Section
R5a72	"		Centrepaire	
R5c33 - R5d87	"		Dugout openings	
G31b00 - G31b96	"		Digging engine house Trench for sumppump — the one supplied by Corps being unsuitable. Being prepared for installation.	
R5d03 - R5a37	"		Centrepaire	} 1 Section
R5c45 - R5a55	"		do. 2 ems Infantry (170)	
R5a55 - L5c83	"		do. 1 Coy " (95)	
M1c30	"		do. 1 Coy " (100)	
R5b55	15th		4 Sappers on RST dump	
NAVSTENT Q4c63	"		Trying watchman trib filter	} 1 Section
R5a46	"		Water Supply maintenance	
L5c45 - G31b00	"		Repairing cart/wdgp mains	
G31b00 - G26c42	"		Centrepaire 1 Section + 3S.I. corps	
S27a	"		do. do. Parkthorp IRLES barrels for pans	
R5c33 - R5d87	"		Water Supply	
M1c30	"		do.	
R5a75	"		4 Sappers on RST dump	
R5c45 - R5a15	"		Clearing dugout (6 sappers)	
R5d63 - R5a76	"		Centrepaire 1 Coy Infantry (100) + 4 S.I. corps	
M2c71 - M2d53	"		6 platoon (150) + 6 do. Parrots for pans	

Army Form C. 2118.

WAR DIARY
or
INTELLIGENCE SUMMARY
(Erase heading not required.)

92nd Divn & RE. Sheet 5.

Place	Date	Hour	Summary of Events and Information	Remarks and references to Appendices
R22d41 - R14c53	16th		Water supply maintenance } 1 Section	
R5a46	"		Repairing windchiefs on river }	
R5c33 - R5d87	"		Water Supply	
R5a44 - R5a55	"		" road repair	
Miraumont - Pys	"		do + 1 Coy Infantry (100)	
Pys - Cemetery	"		do + 3 Coys do. (300)	
R7c55	"		} + 75 S. wagons	
R5a7-	"		Tilting dugout for Officers Shelter	
R5d c30	"		Repairing dugout	
R5c33, R6d35	17th		Within carpentership (4+ sappers)	
R22d44 - R14c53	"		Water supply	
			(parties) } 2 Shelters Chatons	
Miraumont - Pys			Roadrepair	1 Section + 1 Battn infantry (360) + 10 S.S. wagons
Petit Miraumont			Manhole dugouts from Miraumont Cellars	1 Sectn pltn
R10 a 43			water dumps (4 sappers)	
L71 c 30			Pitching tents watertank	1 Sectn platoon + 2 platoon Inf.
Miraumont - Icles	18th		Road repair	do
R5 a	"		Water supply	2 do.
Miraumont, Icles	"		Tentch supply (4 sappers)	
L71 c 30				Machine moved up Miraumont - Icles road
Achiet le Grand	19th		Reconnaissance Junction - complete route from 3 ration convoys	Miraumont Hielle. Sept 3 bridges wagon names
Miraumont - Pys	"		Roadrepair	1 Sect platoon + 2 coys Inf + 45 S.S. wagons
Petit Miraumont	"		do.	do
Icles - Icles	"		water supply	+ 2 coys Inf (115)
Petit Miraumont	"		Manhole from HESSIAN }	
Micr33 - Icles	"		water supply	
Puchet le Grand	"		2 chain HELIGE Phones trailers Wt. Signature cable	
L71 c 30			2449. Wt. W14957/M90 750,000 1/16 J.B.C. &A. Forms/C.2118/12	

Army Form C. 2118.

WAR DIARY
or
INTELLIGENCE SUMMARY
(Erase heading not required.)

Instructions regarding War Diaries and Intelligence Summaries are contained in F. S. Regs., Part II and the Staff Manual respectively. Title Pages will be prepared in manuscript.

92nd Field Co. R.E.   Sheet 6

Place	Date	Hour	Summary of Events and Information	Remarks and references to Appendices
	March 1917			
	20th		Works same as yesterday. Old Mills. Road through Mailly not passable for traffic.	
			Coy then concentrated marched to MIDLAND HUTS near MARTINSART — Supper tin left in camp & again home at MIRAUMONT	
	21st	10 a.m.	Coy marched from MIDLAND HUTS to WARLOY BAILLON arriving 12.45 p.m.	
	22nd	7 a.m.	Coy marched (under 55th Fld Coy orders) from WARLOY BAILLON to MONTONVILLERS arriving 11.30 a.m.	
	23rd	8.30 a.m.	Transport marched from MONTONVILLERS to SALEUX arriving 12 noon	
			Rest of Coy entrained to SALEUX by train from VILLERS BOCAGE, arriving 1 p.m.	
SALEUX	24th		Inspections & Kit. One Officer & 6 O.R. entrained at SALEUX STA. 6 p.m. to proceed to area for billeting.	
	25th	8.30 a.m.	Coy marched to SALEUX STA.	
		9.15 a.m.	Commenced entraining — camp left 11 a.m.	
		11.30 a.m.	Train left SALEUX.	
STEENBECQUE STA	26th	6.30 p.m.	Train arrived. Detrained & marched away at 7.20 p.m. Arriving in billets at BOESEGHEM at 8.30 p.m.	
BOESEGHEM	27th		Cleaning Coy transport	
	28th		Det. marched to AIRE under O.C. Ice Bridging School	
	29th		Reconnaissance of Brigade area in support of schemes	
	30th		Practice in demolition of Culverts etc. Practice in pontoon drill formations.	
	31st		Anti Gas respirators & helmets examined & whole Coy passed through chamber of lachrymatory gas.	
			Casualties during month	
	1st		One Officer joined as reinforcement	
	6th		1 O.R. Transferred to 138th A.T. Coy R.E.	
	9th		8 L.D. Horses arrived as reinforcements	
	15th		5 O.R. wounded in Action — 3 evacuated	
	16th		1 L.D. Horse evacuated to 6.30" M.V.S.	
			1 O.R. wounded in Action	

Army Form C. 2118.

WAR DIARY
~~INTELLIGENCE SUMMARY~~
(Erase heading not required.)

Instructions regarding War Diaries and Intelligence Summaries are contained in F. S. Regs., Part II. and the Staff Manual respectively. Title Pages will be prepared in manuscript.

Sheet No 4

Place	Date	Hour	Summary of Events and Information	Remarks and references to Appendices
	17th		2 Mules arrived as reinforcements	
	18th		1 L.D. Horse evacuated to 3.0-M.V.S.	
	25th		19 O.R. joined from Base as reinforcements	
	29th		1 L.D. Horse shot by V.O.	
	31st		2 O.R. joined as reinforcements	

Portman Capt. RE
for O.C. 92nd Field Co RE.

WAR DIARY or INTELLIGENCE SUMMARY

Army Form C. 2118.

92nd Field Co RE   Sheet No. 1   Vol 2

Place	Date	Hour	Summary of Events and Information	Remarks and references to Appendices
BOESEGHEM	April 1917			
	1st		Coy had baths in AIRE 9.30 am - 11.30 am. Kit inspection. One Pontoon wagon sent to fetch Pontoon equipment left at LEPLEISIEL on January 12th. Football in afternoon. Voluntary Cafe Service in evening.	
	2nd		G.O.C. Division inspected Coy at training in morning. Drill, musketry, bayonet fighting, trestle bridging. All Section out on night scheme 9pm – 1am – laying out assembly trenches.	
	3rd		One Section brought Pontoon equipment from 1st Pontoon Park at MOLINGHEM to canal near AIRE. Two sections trestle bridging. One Section dismantling old trestle bridge near STEENBECQUE STATION. R.E. football team defeated 11th R. Fusiliers 3-1 in afternoon. 4 men of 92nd Co. playing, 3 from 79th Co. & 4 from 80th Co.	
	4th		All four sections practising pontoon bridging on canal near AIRE.	
	5th		Same as yesterday. In afternoon RE football team defeated 6th Northants 4-0 in 2nd Round Div. Tournament.	
	6th		Coy practising pontoon & trestle bridging in morning. Strong point scheme at night.	
	7th		Coy out on route march all day.	
	8th		Kit inspection.	
	9th		RE team 9.30 (6 min from 92nd Co) joined 2nd place in Div. 10 mile cross country race. Coy doing musketry, drill & bayonet fighting in morning. RE team drew 1-1 with Etrangers in 3rd Round Div. Football Tournament. After extra 40 mins. In Div! Best Turn out competition 92nd Co. took 1st prize pack jump.	
	10th		Training in musketry, rapid wiring, bayonet fighting. Etrangers team RE. 2-1 in play off 3rd Round Div Tournament.	
	11th		Training in musketry, bayonet fighting, trestle bridging, rapid wiring.	
	12th, 13th		Training in rapid wiring, bayonet fighting, trestle bridging, musketry, drill.	
	14th		Route march.	
	15th		Kit inspection & baths for 2 sections.	

Army Form C. 2118.

WAR DIARY or INTELLIGENCE SUMMARY
(Erase heading not required.)

92nd Field Co. R.E.   Sheet 2.

Place	Date	Hour	Summary of Events and Information	Remarks and references to Appendices
	April 1917			
BOESEGHEM	16th	10 a.m.	Inspection of Coy in marching order by CE 2nd Corps.	
	17th		Coy training – Bayonet fighting, trestle bridging. Repairing 55th Bde transport.	
	18th		Coy training – trestle bridging. Repairing Bde transport. Baths for 1 Section at AIRE	
	19th		Trestle bridging, competition between Sections. Live Cabin trestle wagons, out 3 bay trestle bridge across Canal, dismantle trestle wagons – 50 minutes. Inspections of Anti Gas appliances 11.30 a.m.	
	20th	9.25 a.m.	Coy marched in 55th–13th Group to LAMBRES arriving 11.30 a.m.	
LAMBRES	21st	8.0 a.m.	Coy marched in 55th Bde Group to BETHUNE arriving 2.30 pm – attached XI Corps	
BETHUNE	22nd		Kit inspection, relieving wagons	
	23rd	5.30 pm	Coy marched from BETHUNE to PETIT SERVINS arriving 9.40 pm	
PETIT SERVINS	24th	10.45 a.m.	Coy marched from PETIT SERVINS to AUX RIETZ (near NEUVILLE ST. VAAST) arriving 2.15 pm. attached II Can. Div. for ration purposes.	
AUX RIETZ	25th	7 am–4 pm	Coy worked on light railways for ADLR under Canadian Rife Co. in NEUVILLE ST VAAST area.	
	26th 27th		} Same as 25th	
	28th	9.30 a.m.	Coy marched from AUX RIETZ to BERURAINS arriving 1.30 pm. York nr Ecurures & 7/200th Field Co.	
			Coy came under orders of 78th Div. again	
	29th		Improving bivouac, kit inspection	
	30th	7.30 am–5 pm	Coy worked on road NEUVILLE VITASSE – ST. MARTIN clearing & earth filling.	

Army Form C. 2118.

WAR DIARY
or
INTELLIGENCE SUMMARY
(Erase heading not required.)

Sheet No. 3

Instructions regarding War Diaries and Intelligence Summaries are contained in F. S. Regs., Part II. and the Staff Manual respectively. Title Pages will be prepared in manuscript.

Place	Date	Hour	Summary of Events and Information	Remarks and references to Appendices
Boesinghem	1-4-17		Casualties during month	
"	5-4-17		3 O.R. arrived as reinforcement from base	
"	"		3 O.R " " "	
"	6-4-17		2 Light Draft Horses shot by Veterinary Officer	
"	"		2 " " evacuated to M.V.S.	
"	10-4-17		1 O.R. joined from Hospital as reinforcement	
"	2-4-17		1 O.R. evacuated to M.C.C.S.	
"	12-4-17		2 O.R. joined as reinforcements from base	
"	16-4-17		10 O.R. transferred to R.E. R.C.C.	
Bethune	23-4-17		2 O.R. joined as reinforcement from 7th Reinforcement Coy R.E.	
Aux Rietz	26-4-17		3 O.R. evacuated to 1st N.C.C.S.	
Beaurains	30-4-17		2 O.R " " C.C.S.	

P.N. Munn
for O.C. 92 nd Capt R.E.
& late 6 R.E.

WAR DIARY or INTELLIGENCE SUMMARY

(Erase heading not required.)

Army Form C. 2118.

92nd Field Coy RE Sheet I Vol 2

Place	Date	Hour	Summary of Events and Information	Remarks and references to Appendices
	May 1917			
	1st	7 am	HQrs and Sections with Tool Carts moved from BEAURAINS to Hindenburg trenches at N.28.c.04. Transport under spare officer moved to N.25.d.78. (NEUVILLE VITASSE – HENIN SUR COJEUL road) Dugouts being made for Battn. HQ. at N.30.b.65½ and Btln HQ report centre at N.30.b.62. Forward R.E. dumps being formed at HENNEL and O.25.d.55. Four Platoons – Strength 27 each – attached to Coy from today. 8th Jerseys to No.1 Section. 7th Queens to No.2 Section. 7th Buffs to No.3 Section. 7th R.W.Kents to No.4 Section. One O.R. 7th Buffs Killed.	
	2nd		Work on dugouts &c as yesterday. Reconnaissance of trenches by all officers.	
	3rd		No.1, 2 & 3 Sections Platoons under new scheme staked shing points at O.34.c.09, O.33.b.53, O.27.d.64. That section to make entry point in CHERISY & subsidiary strong points in O.27.c. Owing to other being unsuccessful, parties were not able to get forward, returned to camp 3 pm. At 10.30 pm the Coy were ordered to men switchline and in N.22.d to repel enemy counterattack coming down COJEUL river – attack did not develop & Coy returned to camp 12.30 am 4th.	
	5th		4 dugouts started in trench N.30.c. You suchona ch/65. (BOOTHAM TRENCH)	
	6th		Work as yesterday. 2 killed & 2 wounded OR. 92nd Coy. 1 killed OR 7th Buffs.	
	7th–16th		Work on dugouts as yesterday. At night one battalion digging new cable trench alongside ... working west for first kms at O.25.d.40.	
	9th		Work on dugouts as yesterday. One battalion at night filing in old trenches in N.30.d. in front of BOOTHAM trench.	
	16th		Work on dugouts as yesterday. Also working in front of BOOTHAM TRENCH. All entrances now down to their full depth of 22 frames – (9 inch spaced upright) for the steps which is 45° & horizontal. Samples taken of all walls in	
	17th			

Army Form C. 2118.

Instructions regarding War Diaries and Intelligence Summaries are contained in F. S. Regs., Part II. and the Staff Manual respectively. Title Pages will be prepared in manuscript.

WAR DIARY
or
INTELLIGENCE SUMMARY
(Erase heading not required.)

92nd Field Co. R.E.

Sheet 2

Place	Date	Hour	Summary of Events and Information	Remarks and references to Appendices
	May 1917			
			HENINEL, numbering 25 Sapper and 1 C.R.E. All but three are fit for duty, with slight	
			alleviation. Also Gothamen Billet at N.35 d 67. Scheme prepared & forwarded for Divl. Baths at N.33 b/6	N.33 b/6
	12th		Work on dugouts as before. 2 Corps infantry employed at filling trenches in N.30 d.	
	13th		Work on dugouts	
	14th		Work on dugouts. A Coys. Middlesex Regt filling in trenches N.30 d.	
	15th		Work on dugouts	
	16th		Work on dugouts. 150 Infantry clearing & deepening BOOTHAM TRENCH	
	17th		Work on dugouts	
	18th		Work on dugouts. 2 completed. Work on BOOTHAM TRENCH	
	19th		Work on 2 dugouts; renewing 2 completed. Work on BOOTHAM TRENCH. Erecting baths N.33 b.48. 100 Infantry	
			deepening BOOTHAM Trench.	
	20th		Took over work from 79th Field Co. R.E. Work on baths. Work on CONCRETE TRENCH	
	21st		Hot Pet on dugout at 031 a 23, ho 2 273 Scheme changing over. New on dugout 031 C.49.	
	22nd & 23rd 12th		ho 1 " " ho 2 73 " 10th infantry deepening new frontline. New on dugout 031 C.49.	
	25th		ho 1 " " ho 2 on dugout 031 b 27 commenced, ho 3 Pln with 100 Infantry chipping	
			at STOCK ENDED Trenches.	
	26, 27th & 28th		ho 1 on dugout 031 a 23, ho 2 on dugout 031 b 27, ho 3 Section using frames, new etc. 200 Infantry digging at WOOD lane.	
	29th		do " ho 3 on dugout N.36 b 2 to 5, ho 4 on dugout N.21c.04 & 100 Inf.y digging PELICAN LANE	
	30th		do " do " 9/10 Infantry digging POTTENDEN & PELICAN LANE	
	31st		do " do " do	

Contributor Ref. diff.y 031C18 - 031C59, 2 Platoon diff.y 031C86 - 031C64, 2 Platoon diff.y 031C86 - 031C64, 2 Platoon diff.y 031C86 - 031C25.
3 platoon diff.y 051 dc3 - 01b59.

2449 Wt. W14957/M90 750,000 1/16 J.B.C. & A. Forms/C.2118/12.

Army Form C. 2118.

WAR DIARY
or
INTELLIGENCE SUMMARY

(Erase heading not required.)

Sheet No. III

Place	Date	Hour	Summary of Events and Information	Remarks and references to Appendices
	2-5-17		1 O.R evacuated to C.C.S.	
	3-5-17		2 O.R wounded in action	
	5-5-17		5 O.R evacuated to C.C.S	
	6-5-17		2 O.R killed in action	
			1 O.R wounded in action remains at duty	
			1 O.R wounded in action	
	10-5-17		1 O.R joined as reinforcement from hospital	
	12-5-17		1 O.R	
	15-5-17		2nd Lieut V. Wilkins R.E. left to report to C.R.E. ETAPLES	
			transfer from 7th Royal West Kent Regt.	
	17-5-17		1 O.R joined as reinforcement	
			2nd Lieut G. Neely R.E. joined as reinforcement from Base	
	21-5-17		1 O.R joined as reinforcement	
	26-5-17		2nd Lieut Patman wounded, injured	
	27-5-17		4 Light Draft Horses joined	
	31-5-17		1 O.R rejoined as reinforcement from base	

P. Crimmin Capt R.E.
O. C. 92nd Field Co R.E.

Army Form C. 2118.

Vol 23

92nd Field Coy R.E.

Sheet I

WAR DIARY or INTELLIGENCE SUMMARY
(Erase heading not required.)

Place	Date	Hour	Summary of Events and Information	Remarks and references to Appendices
Sector facing HINDENBURG	June 1917			
	1st		No.1 Section (attached to Sussex platoon) commenced emplacement elongate for heavy T.M. (V.18 T.M.B) at O25 d10	
			No.2 " 7" Buffs " continuing work on dugout for Left Coy HQrs at O31 b27 in CURTAIN TRENCH	
			No.3 " 7" Queens " " " for Batln. HQ. at N36 b2505 in AVENUE TRENCH.	
			No.4 " 7" Queens " " " for Fd Coy HQ at N28 c04 in HINDENBURG LANE	
			All working 3 Shifts. Materials brought up nightly by Coy transport to N30 c71 & carried forward by Infantry Platoons.	
			At night One Officer & 2 Platoons 7" Queens digging new trench from WREN LANE O31 b55 to new post at O31 b82 immediately after capture of (latter). 2 NCOs & 7" Southwarks & 7" Queens wiring in front of new posts at O31 b34 and O31 b89 at same time.	
			Also One Officer & 4 Platoons 12" Middlesex digging out WOOD TRENCH.	
	2nd		Sections worked as yesterday. At night One Officer & 6 Platoons Suffolks getting wiring materials forward	
	3rd		Letters worked as yesterday. In addition new Set. supplied 6 sappers to work & & 2nd RGA making dugout for 60 pdr battery at N28 c23.	
	4th		Same as 3rd.	
	5th		Sections worked as before. At night One Officer & 6 Completion 7" Bedfords digging out communication trench from PELICAN LANE to CURTAIN TRENCH O31 c25 – O31 c58, and 3 platoons 7" Bedfords digging out communication Trench in ROTTEN ROW connecting STORM TRENCH TRENCHES, O31 c64 – O31 c52.	
	6th		Sections worked as for 5th. At night one officer & 3 platoons 7" Bedfords digging out STORM TRENCH (SW of LARK LANE), and SWALLOW LANE.	

WAR DIARY or INTELLIGENCE SUMMARY

Army Form C. 2118.

(Erase heading not required.)

Place: 92nd Field Coy. R.E.
Sheet 2.

Date	Hour	Summary of Events and Information	Remarks and references to Appendices
June 1917			
7th		Sections worked as for 6th. At night 4 platoons 6th Northants under sacrifices digging at STORK TRENCH and SWALLOW LANE and making fire step in Entr. at O31d cent'd.	
8th		Sections worked as for 7th. No.2 Completed thin dugout at O31b27, 36'×9'×20' feet ends. Also repaired and strengthened entrance of dugout in CURTAIN TRENCH at O31a83, and one booby trapped & hunted out dugout at night and 4 plns 11/C & 3 platoons 7th Bedfords digging out WOOD TRENCH.	
9th		Sections worked as for 8th. At night 6 platoons 7th Bedfords & M.G.s digging new trench from O31a89 to O31c83. Cut heavy enemy barrage restrained work parts & hardly any work done.	
10th		No.1 Sect onwards work as before. No.2 Sect took over dugout at N28c23 from No.4 Section & also started making approach pieces for shell-holes. No.3 Sect onwards work as before. No.4 Sect started new dugout for 14 O.R. Coy 1/Q.S. in TURLLON LANE at O31c7560.	
11th		Sections worked as yesterday. At night 4 platoons 6th Northants digging at N.E. end of STORK TRENCH and 2 platoons widening trench from PELICAN LANE to CURTAIN TRENCH	
12th		Sections worked as yesterday. No.2 began fixing frames at advanced post in JOINT TRENCH. At night 2 platoons worked at WOOD TRENCH.	
13th		All Section work as yesterday. No.3 Completed new Bn. H.Q. in AVENUE TRENCH. At night 2 platoons of 6th Northants digging WOOD TRENCH.	
14th		No.1 Section on same work (T.M.B. emplacement etc.) No.2 " " (Splinter proof shelter for sentry posts in finished.) 2 gunner dugout at N28 c23. No.3 " Began making new dugout in STORK TRENCH at O31a55 for Left Coy. H.Q. No.4 " same dugout at O31c76. At night 4 platoons 6th Northants widening PELICAN LANE.	

2449. Wt. W14957/M90 750,000 1/16 J.B.C. & A. Forms/C.2118/12.

Army Form C. 2118.

WAR DIARY
or
INTELLIGENCE SUMMARY
(Erase heading not required.)

92nd Field Coy R.E.

Sheet No. 3

Place	Date	Hour	Summary of Events and Information	Remarks and references to Appendices
			June 1917	
	15th		All Section work same as yesterday. At night the trench was going to be dug from junction of STORK TRENCH and ARZEN LANE to dugout in CABLE TRENCH, by 7 platoon workouts, but Major Haynen was hit whilst laying out tapes & no one else knew ground & details, parties were dismissed	
	16th		All Section work same as yesterday. In morning took round actg. Officer trenches 67 and 7th Co. who arrived last night to relieve this Coy. Handed on all plans & documents.	
	17th	3.40am	Coy marched to hutted camp S.E. of COIGNEUX arriving 12 noon.	
COIGNEUX	18th		Rifle and kit inspections.	
	19th, 20th		Coy resting	
	21st	2pm	Coy marched to SAULTY Station (halting 2hrs for tea at HUMBLINCOURT) arriving 7.30pm. Began entraining	
		10pm	completed 11pm. (One Coy Pioneers also on train together with 2 two the wagon (1 Batn Yd Corps.)	
			One Officer, 12 ORs. and 2 horses. Left at COIGNEUX for training 55th 2/15th in evening, leaving to	
	22nd	2am	Train left SAULTY arriving HOPOUTRE siding (POPERINGHE) 11.30 am. Marched on then	
			arrived at 1.05pm to camp near BUSSEBOOM at G.20 b.28. (Sheet 28).	
	23rd		Resting in quarters for 2nd Corps	
HOOGEGRAAF OPID.	24th		do	
	25th			
	26th		and arriving 1.45 & 7th Co. 10.30pm 2nd Corps workshops	
	27th			
	28th		"Dismantling old 2 Horse My booth in laundry fact" corps	
	29th			
	30th			

R.S. Knightape
O.C. 92 Field Co RE

Army Form C. 2118.

WAR DIARY
or
INTELLIGENCE SUMMARY
(Erase heading not required.)

Sheet No 4

Place	Date	Hour	Summary of Events and Information	Remarks and references to Appendices
			CASUALTIES	
	1-6-17		2 O.R. joined as reinforcements	
			1 O.R. killed in action. 2.O.R wounded in action.	
	2-6-17		2.O.R. killed in action. 1 O.R wounded in action	
	14-6-17		Major W.M. Hayman D.S.O. R.E. wounded in action	
	19-6-17		1 O.R transferred to 12th D well R.E.A.R.	
	20-6-17		2nd Lieut A.S. Beecroft R.E. joined as reinforcement from the Base.	
	26-6-17		6 O.R. joined as reinforcements	
	29-6-17		Capt R.E. Knight R.E. 92th Field Co. R.E. assumed command of the Co. by during the absence, on leave, of Major Nunn R.E.	

R S Knight Capt R.E.
O.C. 92nd Field Co. R.E.

WAR DIARY or INTELLIGENCE SUMMARY

Army Form C. 2118.

(Erase heading not required.)

92nd Field Coy RE

Stamp: 92nd (FIELD) COMPANY ROYAL ENGINEERS

July 1917

Place	Date	Hour	Summary of Events and Information	Remarks and references to Appendices
BUSSEBOOM	1st		Erecting new 2nd Corps Camp. Dismantling old camp. Assisting 145 A.T.C. in Corps Workshop. 1 Section in Training	
	2nd		" " " "	
	3rd		(Road line with CRE and OC 80th Y(M) RE) Erecting new 2nd Corps Camp. Dismantling old camp. Assisting 145 A.T.C. 1 Section Training	
	4th		Erecting new 2nd Corps Camp. Dismantling 146 A.T.O. 1 Section Training.	
	5th		" " " "	
	6th		Company moved to H.26.b.3.1. approx. leaving Bussebeem 10 a.m. Road Recce with OC 201st Coy RE at 4 am. Advance Camp at H.26.b.3.1. 4 Sections and OC left H.26.b.5.1. at 3 am. with necessary transport and took over Billets and work 720 1st/406 RE. Pyro - Transport and Horse Lines - CSM and Office remained at formed Camp under Lt Griffiths RE. New recess getting into Billets etc. Evening	
ZILLEBEKE BUND	7th		Section Officers and Recce round work. Self to Bde.	
	8th		Started continuous shifts on Dressing Station on Ritz Street - Bde Hqrs Wellington Crescent - Regimental Aid Post off Vince St.	
	9th		Road line with CRE	1 Section casns from mustard gas burns underground shelter at Zillebeke Bund.
	10th		Work on Zillebeke - Bodmin Lane tramline - Dressing Station on Ritz St - Bde Hqrs in Wellington Crescent - RAP off Vince St - Shelter in Zillebeke Bund.	
	11th		Draining up pulling Bodmin Lane and Kincott.	
	12th		" " " " Bde Hqrs in Wellington Crescent completed - RAP off Vince	
	13th		Marking out and digging new trench from Maple Trench to Starling St. Ritz St Dressing Station. Maple Trench Dressing Station. Vince St Dressing Station. Shelter in Zillebeke Bund.	
	14th		" " " "	
	15th		" " " "	
	16th		" " " "	Cutaway track for gunners. Repairs to Zillebeke tramline.
	17th		" " " "	
	18th		2 Dressing Stns Maple Trench. Vince St Dressing Station. Shelter in Zillebeke Bund. Bde bomb store Zillebeke Bund. Bde bomb store at Zillebeke Church. 14th HY pros Push in trench.	Marking out forward trench as parallel as possible.
	19th		" " completed	" Bde bomb store Zillebeke Church
	20th		" " extended	" " "
	21st		" " completed, Vince St RAP, Dressing Stn, Billets in Zillebeke Bund.	abandoned
	22nd		" " " "	by order 30th Div
	23rd		Zillebeke Bund dug outs for Officers. Tunnel blocked for own cavalry track repaired	

WAR DIARY
or
INTELLIGENCE SUMMARY

Army Form C. 2118.

(Erase heading not required.)

92 Field Coy R.E.   July 1917

Place	Date	Hour	Summary of Events and Information	Remarks and references to Appendices
DICKEBUSCH	24-7-17		4 Sections & 4 attached Inf. Platoons moved from ZILLEBEKE BUND at 4am arrived at DICKEBUSCH at 6am. Camp was formed & equipment & transport cleaned.	
	25-7-17		Work commenced on 54 pairs of private carriers & 20 attachments for G.S. saddle. 4 Sections & attached Inf. Infantry training.	
	26-7-17		54 pairs private carriers & 20 attachments for G.S. saddle completed. " "	
	27-7-17		Coy & attached Inf. Baths in morning. Training in afternoon.	
	28-7-17		4 Sections & attached Infantry. Training in morning. Sports were held in the afternoon.	
	29-7-17		Half day. Company and attached Inf. paraded for chief parade etc. Attaches for C.R.E. completed.	
	30-7-17		Paraded for Company and attached Infantry in fighting order. Mounted Sgt. his Cpl. and 10 Drivers with Pack Animals reported to O.C. Bn C. Arm. I took accompanied them. Lt. Paterson R.E. and Water Party left for ZILLEBEKE BUND at 6pm.	
	31-7-17		Chief Parade. Company standing by ready to move at short notice.	

Casualties during Month

2nd Lieut C.N. Ranyland joined as reinforcement from Base

	10-7-17		2nd Lieut C.N. Ranyland joined as reinforcement	
	13-7-17		2 O.Rs wounded in action	
	13-7-17		1 O.R. joined as reinforcement.	
	15-7-17		1 O.R. killed and 3 O.Rs wounded in action	
	16-7-17		1 Light Draft Horse killed by Shell Fire.	
	17-7-17		1 " " wounded	
	20-7-17		1 O.R. killed in action.	
			1 Light Draft Horses killed by Shell Fire.	
			4 " " arrived as reinforcement from 18" Divl Ammunition Column	
	21-7-17		1 O.R. wounded in action	
			1 Light Draft Horse evacuated to 30th M.V.S.	
	24-7-17		6 " " arrived as reinforcements	
	26-7-17		1 O.R. joined as reinforcement from Base	
	28-7-17		7 O.Rs " " No 6 Reinforcement Coy. R.E.	
	29-7-17		1 O.R. accidentally injured and evacuated	

R. Knight Capt R.E.
for O. Comdg 92nd (Fd.) Co. R.E.

WAR DIARY
or
INTELLIGENCE SUMMARY

Army Form C. 2118.

92nd Field Coy RE

V 6125

Place	Date	Hour	Summary of Events and Information	Remarks and references to Appendices
DICKEBUSCH	1.8.17		Coy + attached platoons in Divisional Reserve	Wet
	2.8.17		Training	"
	3.8.17		"	
ZILLEBEKE-BUND	4.8.17	4.30am	3 Sections + attached platoons moved to ZILLEBEKE BUND. Reconnaissance of Front line system by Officers & Sgts.	
	5.8.17		" " " " Carrying material for strong points. 1 Section training at DICKE BUSCH.	
	6.8.17		" " " " making strong points, " " "	
	7.8.17		" " " " forming forward R.E. dumps & points of assembly. Pumping at cleaning SP. " "	
	8.8.17		" " " " " " " " " " " " Section training	
	9.8.17		1 Section making joining point. 2 Sections + attached platoons forming forward dumps & R.E. stores. 1 " "	
	10.8.17		1 " " " " " " " " " "	
	11.8.17		1 " " " " " Bde Reserve 1 Section training	
			1 " deepening JASPER AV. 1 Section deepening JAP AV. 1 Section - 3 Sections and 3 Platoons returned to Coy Hqrs at DICKEBUSCH.	
DICKEBUSCH	12.8.17		Check Parade - Cleaning Company Equipment.	
	13.8.17		Company moved from Dickebush to L25a 2.2 (huts) near ABEELE. Attached Platoons rejoined this Coy.	
ABEELE	14.8.17		Check Parade for fitting equipment and route march. Advance party by lorry to ZEGGERS-CAPEL.	
	15.8.17		Company entrained at ABEELE 6·30am and detrained at ESQUELBECQ 9am marched to T29 d 2·8 (Shutiques) near ZEGGERS-CAPEL. Transport 1746000	
SPRENN-KOT	16.8.17		Check Parade - cleaning up.	
"	17.8.17		Training	
MILLAIN	18.8.17		moved to MILLAIN. Whole Company by Road. Work for 2nd Corps Infantry School	
"	19.8.17		Work for 2nd Corps Infantry School	
	20.8.17		" " " "	
	21.8.17		" " " "	
	22.8.17		" " " "	
	23.8.17		" " " "	
	24.8.17		" " " "	
	25.8.17		" " " "	
	26.8.17		" " " "	
	27.8.17		" " " "	
	28.8.17		" " " "	
	29.8.17		" " " "	
	30.8.17		" " " "	
	31.8.17		" " " "	

R.P. Knight Capt RE
for O.C. 92nd Field Co. RE

WAR DIARY or INTELLIGENCE SUMMARY

(Erase heading not required.) Sheet No. 2

Army Form C. 2118.

Place	Date	Hour	Summary of Events and Information	Remarks and references to Appendices
			Casualties	
	1-8-17		1 O.R. joined as reinforcement from Base	
	4-8-17		1 O.R. killed in action	
	"		2 L.D. horses arrived as reinforcements	
	6-8-17		2 other Ranks wounded in action	
	7-8-17		1 O.R. joined as reinforcement from the Base	
	7-8-17		1 O.R. wounded in action	
	10-8-17		2nd Lieut. W. Paterson R.E. killed in action	
	13-8-17		Lieut. Beattie R.E. left to join 5th Army School Staff	
	12-8-17		4 O.R. joined as reinforcements from No. 6 Reinforcement Co.	
	9-8-17		L/Cpl Miller awarded the Military Medal	
	20-8-17		2nd Lieut James R.E. joined as reinforcement from Base	
	22-8-17		1 L.D. horse arrived as reinforcement	

R. S. Knight Capt. R.E.
for O.C. 92nd Field Co., R.E.

Army Form C. 2118.

WAR DIARY
or
INTELLIGENCE SUMMARY

92nd Field Company R.E.
Sheet N° 1

(Erase heading not required.)

Place	Date	Hour	Summary of Events and Information	Remarks and references to Appendices
MILLAM	1-9-17		Work for 2nd Corps Infantry School. Two Sections training.	
	2		"	
	3		"	
	4		"	
	5		"	
	6		"	
	7		"	
	8		"	
	9		"	
	10		"	
	11		"	
	12		"	
	13		"	
	14		"	
	15		"	
SPRENNKOT	16		Company rejoined Division marching to SPRENNKOT (cross roads about 1 mile NE of ZEGGERS-CAPEL Sheet 5A)	
	17		Company training.	
	18		"	
	19		"	
	20		"	
	21		"	
	22		"	
	23		"	
	24		"	
	25		"	
	26		"	
	27		"	
BRIELEN	28		Dismounted portion of Coy moved to BRIELEN area B30a 9.7 Sheet 28 NW by Bus. Transport by road to Horse Lines in POPERINGHE Area at A2 8 a 8.7.	
	29		Round the work with C.R.E. and Section officers.	
	30		Started work on camp for 1 Field Coy and its attached Platoon. Also repair of forward Roads. 2 Attached Platoons joined.	

Army Form C. 2118.

WAR DIARY
or
INTELLIGENCE SUMMARY

(Erase heading not required.) Sheet No. 2

Instructions regarding War Diaries and Intelligence Summaries are contained in F. S. Regs., Part II. and the Staff Manual respectively. Title Pages will be prepared in manuscript.

Place	Date	Hour	Summary of Events and Information CASUALTIES	Remarks and references to Appendices
	4-9-17		One O.R. joined as reinforcement from Base	
	5-9-17		Two O.R's " " " " " "	
	8-9-17		Two " " " " " " Base	
	11-9-17		Capt L. Grice R.E. and 1 O.R. attached from 5th Army School	
	9-9-17		2nd Lieut. J.R. Bailey R.E. joined as reinforcement	
	16-9-17		Three O.R's joined as reinforcements from Base	
	24-9-17		Two O.R's evacuated to Base	
	24-9-17		Four O.R's evacuated to C.C.S.	
	29-9-17		One O.R. joined as reinforcement from Base	

R.V. Knight Capt R.E.
for O.C. 92 in Field Coy R.E.

WAR DIARY or INTELLIGENCE SUMMARY

Army Form C. 2118.

92nd Sec RE 28 Vol 27

(Erase heading not required.)

for October 1917.

Place	Date	Hour	Summary of Events and Information	Remarks and references to Appendices
BRIELEN	1-10-17		3 sections and attached Platoons working on forward dump for field Company and attached Platoon at C.15.b.08. 1 section and attached Platoon on repair of FARM ROAD (C.4a.32) and horry diversion for same.	
B30a77	2		"	
Hut 28NN	3		"	
	4		"	
	5		"	
	6		"	
	7		"	
	8		"	
	9		"	
	10		2 sections and attached Platoons moved to forward Billets at C.15.B.08	
	11		2 sections and attached Platoons continue work on forward dump at C.15.b.08; 2 sections and attached Platoons commenced work on duckboard track from PHEASANT FARM to POELCAPELLE (Reference 40,000) Trench map POELCAPELLE)	
	12		forming forward Dump for consolidation and strong Points	
	13		2 sections and attached Platoons started by for forming Strong Points, remainder on Duckboard. Company and attached Platoons on duckboard track from PILCKEM RD to PATHy POELCAPELLE.	
	14		"	
	15		"	
	16		"	
	17		"	
	18		"	
	19		"	
	20		"	
	21		"	
	22		"	
	23		"	
	24		"	
	25		"	
	26		Company and attached Platoons moved to HOSPITAL FARM, Bigd It sheet 28."	
	27		Coy moved to C.13.a.3.5 sheet 28 to relieve 93rd Fd Coy RE on work on tramline in U.22 a & b (Burghoote). Attached Platoons rejoined Bn	
	28		work on Tramways for 157 Bde RFA in U.22.a & b (Burgkotte) Horses lines moved to A.11.a.9.4. (Sheet 28). 50 Cavalry attached.	
	29			
	30			
	31			

2449 Wt. W14957/M90 750,000 1/16 J.B.C. & A. Forms/C.2118/12.

Army Form C. 2118.

WAR DIARY
or
INTELLIGENCE SUMMARY Book N° 2

(Erase heading not required.)

Place	Date	Hour	Summary of Events and Information	Remarks and references to Appendices
[illeg]	15.10.17		East Africa	
	19.10.17		1. O.R killed in action 2. O.R's wounded in action	
	23.10.17		40. O.R's joined from the Base as reinforcements	
	23.10.17		2. O.R's joined " " "	
	25.10.17		1. O.R wounded in action	
	27.10.17		Capt. Goldicutt R.E and 2. O.R's wounded in action	
	27.10.17		1. D. Leave Grant	
	22.10.17		1. O.R joined as reinforcement	

R. Murphy Capt. RE
O.C. 93F. Coy. RE

Army Form C. 2118.

WAR DIARY
or
INTELLIGENCE SUMMARY

92nd Field Co R.E.

(Erase heading not required.)

Place	Date	Hour	Summary of Events and Information	Remarks and references to Appendices
C.13.a.2.3 Reference BIXSCHOOTE HAMPTON CAMP	1-11-17		Tramline in U.22.a & b. for 157 Bde. R.F.A.	November 1917. Vol 28
"	2		" " " " " " "	
"	3		" " " " " " "	
"	4		" " " " " " "	
"	5		Company rejoined Division and moved to HAMPTON CAMP - B.11.a.2.3. Horse lines at A.11.a.9.6. (Sheet 28) and took over work of 204th Fld Co R.E.- 35th Div". Attached Platoon joined.	
"	6		Round the work with O.C. 204th Fld Co R.E., Officers and Section Sergeants. Company employed on Billets.	Bixchoote
Bixchoote	7		Maintenance of light Div tramline from STEENBEEK to railhead in Ney Wood. Extending existing line from NEY WOOD to KOEKUIT. Commenced work on New Forward dump NR. ABRI CAMP. Forming forward dump Parkand Footpath WIDGEN DRIFT. Control of BOESINGHE R.E.Pump. Draining and clearing Pack track NEY WOOD Rd - PANAMA House.	
"	8		" " " " " " "	
"	9		" " " " " " "	
"	10		" " " " " " "	
"	11		" " " " " " "	
"	12		" " " " " " "	
"	13		" " " " " " "	
"	14		Same as for 7th inst. In addition carrying out improvement to 55th Inf Bde H.Q. (Bleuet H.Q., additional dug-in station for 5th F.A.	
"	15		Same as for 18th.	
"	19-22		Maintenance work & construction for tramline made. Coy halftime. Intersection relief.	
"	23rd		Maintenance tramway & tramline. Maintenance & muletrack. Extra. to dump. Repair of screen.	
"	24th		Same as for 24th.	
"	25th		Maintenance of tramline. Tramto KOEKUIT. Maintenance tupair of road through PANAMA HOUSE - KOHLENFELD CAMP.	
"	26th		Contd dump.	
"	27 d		Maintenance of tramline & extension. Work on ABRI camp. Beginning of screen carried to U.6.d.05.70 V.6.b.c.c.40 BIXCHOOTE	
"	28 d		line carrying additional ancillary lighting at B.11.a.2.4. Lev 28.	
"	29 d		line on 27th except at screen overhead.	U.6. d.05.45 to V.6.c.5.1
"	30 d		Maintenance & repair of tramline. 501x camouflage screen erected	U.6. d.05.45 to V.12.d.30.85 } BIXCHOOTE. U.6. d.05.65 to V.6.d.20.40

2449 Wt. W14957/Mg0 750,000 1/16 J.B.C. & A. Forms/C.2118/12.

Army Form C. 2118.

WAR DIARY
or
INTELLIGENCE SUMMARY

(Erase heading not required.) Sheet No 2.

Instructions regarding War Diaries and Intelligence Summaries are contained in F. S. Regs., Part II and the Staff Manual respectively. Title Pages will be prepared in manuscript.

Place	Date	Hour	Summary of Events and Information	Remarks and references to Appendices
			Casualties during month	
	5-11-17		2 other Ranks joined as reinforcements from R.E. Base Depot.	
	6-11-17		2 L.D. Horses evacuated to 57th D. of R., M.V.S.	
	10-11-17		1 other Rank evacuated sick	
	12-11-17		1 L.D. Horse destroyed by Shell Fire.	
	19-11-17		Capt R.E. Knight R.E. left this company to command 79th Field Co R.E.	
	15-11-17		1 other Rank evacuated wounded.	
	23-11-17		2nd Lieut Elliott R.E. proceeds to England on duty to report to War Office.	
	26-1-17		1 other Rank joined as reinforcement from R.E. Base Depot	
	22-11-17		Capt T.C.B. Davis R.E. joined as reinforcement and assumed duties as 2nd in command	

Williams
Major R.E.
O.C. 92nd Field Coy. R.E.

Army Form C. 2118.

WAR DIARY
or
INTELLIGENCE SUMMARY
(Erase heading not required.)

92nd Field Co. R.E.   December 1917

Place	Date	Hour	Summary of Events and Information	Remarks and references to Appendices
Ref. BYSSHOTTE A-JUBTSINGHE 10770	1st		Maintenance tram line from STEENBECK to FOREKUT, and road from NEY onwards to FOREKUT. Contact Y	
	2nd		Div. R.E. Dumps at 190E.1.m.61.H.E. 500 yds screen erected behind outpost line in region of 5 CHEMINS.	
	3rd		Maintenance & control nodes as for 1st. Erecting steering station at CARENTELREEP.	
	4th		do. do. 4 Branch Tramway to same. Plowding	
	5th		do. do. Rodinjour O.16.d.66. U.27.c.2. U.27.a.96 - U.27.b.59. Buildg Shelter	
	6th		Same as 5th. do. Rodinjour O.27.b.25 - U.22.c.01	
	7th		In addition making bridge pedes Hybrailway U.15.d.70 - O.22.a.38.	
	8th		Maintenance control roads as for 1st & erecting Station. Rodinjour TUPES ENDS - LANGEMARCK STN. Also bridge at	
	9th		do. do. do.	
	10th		do. do. do. NEY CROSS Roads repaired. Dist tramway extension Posts OST-OETBERD.	
	11th		do. do. do. Dist tramway extension. Bailey fasten O.11.d.70. O.22.a.38.	
	12th		do. do. do. do. Railway plans spur at 11.b.1.b6	
	13th		Also commenced work on new battery pedes O.21.b.59 to U.15.c.90.	
	14th		Handed over all work to 505th Field Cory R.E. (T.F.) 27th Division.	
	15th		Coy entrained at BOESINGHE 10.45 a.m. Detrained PLOMEN 12.0. Marched to PROVETT CAMP PROVED HEER.	
	16th		Transport road leg 10 a.m. - 11 a.m. - 3 p.m.	
N. PROVEN (HAZEBROUCK Sn.)	17th		Building huts. Latrines. Crushing brams, making cookhouse & under ESCL 19th Capt Scopes	
	18th		" " " " "	
	19th		1 Officer 76 OR sent to drew with 55th Inf Bde for training in using R.E. in MORBASQUET AREA.	
	20th		as 17th. 7 O.R. to 56 per Reel. People	
	21st		" " "	
	22nd			
	23-27			
Nulemp Wirelly 528	4th 5th		Moved to Subsy camp.	
	31st		W 17 pm. 1ft 2 subs V 6 O.R. to 50th Fld Coy. 16 ORs over Rut 27. B.11.a.23.	

WAR DIARY
or
INTELLIGENCE SUMMARY

(Erase heading not required.)

Army Form C. 2118.

Place	Date	Hour	Summary of Events and Information	Remarks and references to Appendices
			Casualties during Month	
	2-12-17		Lieut R Weir RE joined the Company as reinforcement.	
	4-12-17		One L.D. Horse destroyed	
	9-12-17		6 O.R. joined as reinforcements from the Base.	
	15-12-17		2 L.D. Horses arrived as reinforcements	
	17-12-17		One O.R. joined as reinforcement from 47" C.C.S.	
	21-12-17		3 O.R. joined as reinforcement from the Base.	
	28-12-17		1 O.R. evacuated to Base Sick	
	26-12-17		1 O.R. joined as reinforcement from Base.	
			2 O.R. evacuated to Base Sick	

Signed Capt R.E.
O.C 92nd Field Co R.E.

Army Form C. 2118.

WAR DIARY
or
INTELLIGENCE SUMMARY
(Erase heading not required.)

92nd Field Co R.E.

January 1918

Place	Date	Hour	Summary of Events and Information	Remarks and references to Appendices
Shut 19. W.25.b.6.5.	1-1-18.		Erecting huts in Brooding area	
HAMPTON CAMP Shut 28, B.14.a.2.3.	2-1-18.		Move to Hampton camp. horse lines to DE WIPPE CORNER.	
"	3-1-18.		Cleaning up camp & erecting cabin accommodation; interview with O.C. 55 Brigade as to work.	
"	4-1-18.		Reconnaissance of proposed line of wire, from V.5.d.4.2 to V.9.a.7.2 (BROOMBEEK Post) & preparing wire.	
	5-1-18.		Wiring on line as above	
	6-1-18.		" " " "	
	7-1-18.		Work on Abri camp. C.1.b.1.17. Rework on wire as order to 8 Brigade relief.	
	8-1-18.		" " " " Large quantity of material carried to job but too late for work on wire.	
	9-1-18.		" " " " Wiring on line V.5.d.4.2 to V.9.a.7.2. Two sections + two platoons to ABRI camp.	
	10-1-18.		Interview with O.C. 54 Brigade. Wiring on line as above. Line two thirds finished.	
	11-1-18.		(Preparing) wire. 2 work parties to brigade relief. Two sections & two platoons returned to Bdy H.2 from ABRI camp.	
	12-1-18.		(Preparing) wire & pickets. Taping out line of wire in front of posts on our front. Instructing infantry in same.	
	13-1-18.		Wiring front line V.6.a.5.3 to V.6.d.9.8 + V.1.c.7.3 to V.7.b.1.4.	
	14-1-18.		Finishing wire V.1.c.7.3 to V.9.b.1.4. Erecting 3 baby elephant shelters at I"V.12.b.9.2 v.V.6.a.3.2 3at U.15.c.9.3.	
	15-1-18.		Work on E GYPT house. Finishing dugouts as above. + Brigade H.2. U.15.c.9.3. Clearing debris & erecting new dugouts	
	16-1-18.			
	17-1-18.			
	18-1-18.		Re item 17 st. Also enforcing 1500 yds wiring on front line	

Army Form C. 2118.

WAR DIARY
or
INTELLIGENCE SUMMARY
(Erase heading not required.)

Instructions regarding War Diaries and Intelligence Summaries are contained in F. S. Regs., Part II. and the Staff Manual respectively. Title Pages will be prepared in manuscript.

Place	Date	Hour	Summary of Events and Information	Remarks and references to Appendices
HAMPTON CAMP Sheet 26 B.11.a.2.3	20.1.18		Burying Baby Elephant shelters at V.12.b.9.2. Repairs to PASCUAL FARM. Bathhouse ABRI & BABOSA	
	21.1.18		Camp. Also 500 yds. double Apron fence on front line.	
″	22.1.18		Shelters at V.6.d.5.3. 1 Bathhouse. Battalion relief	
″	23.1.18		Constructing shelters at V.5.b.85.25. V.6.a.05.25, V.6.a.2.3. Also dryg/ shelters VEE BEND & PASCUAL FARM	
″	24.1.18		Shelters now finished. Also 2 shelters at V.a.d.8.3. 350 yds double Apron fence on front line. Front line now completed. Arrest with double Apron fence. 2 places not finished.	
″	25.1.18		8. Baby Elephant shelters erected. 4 at VEE BEND. 2 at V.12.d.6.9. 1 at EEGYPT HOUSE	
″	26.1.18		6. ″ 2 at AJAX HOUSE, 1 at CINE CHEMINS. 1 at COLOMBO house. 15	
″	27.1.18		6. B.E. shelters erected about, V.6.c.5.6. Sharp land in 8 posts in left of sector to be fixed by fifth army. 2 Bombodiers at VEE BEND	
″	28.1.18		6. ″ ″	
″	29.1.18		Camp repairs. Baths + Latrines	
″	30.1.18		Move to H. camp. A.9.a.5.4. Sheet 28.	
Sheet 28 A.9.a.54	31.1.18		Move to D.11.c.3.7. Sheet 27.	

2449 Wt. W14957/M90 750,000 1/16 J.B.C. & A. Forms/C.2118/12.

WAR DIARY
or
INTELLIGENCE SUMMARY

Army Form C. 2118.

Place	Date	Hour	Summary of Events and Information	Remarks and references to Appendices
			Casualties during month -	
	3-1-18		2 ORs. joined from RE Base Depot, reinforcements.	
	6-1-18		2 ORs. wounded in action.	
	8-1-18		2 ORs. wounded in action	
	12-1-18		1 OR. joined from RE Base Depot, reinforcement.	
	18-1-18		1 OR reputed missing	
	21-1-18		1 OR. wounded in action	
	23-1-18		2 ORs joined from RE Base Depot, reinforcements	
	28-1-18		1 OR. joined from RE Base Depot, reinforcement.	

Capt R.E.
for O.C. 92nd Field Coy R.E.

Army Form C. 2118.

WAR DIARY
or
INTELLIGENCE SUMMARY

(Erase heading not required.)

92nd Field Coy R.E.

Sheet N°   WD 31

Instructions regarding War Diaries and Intelligence Summaries are contained in F.S. Regs., Part II. and the Staff Manual respectively. Title Pages will be prepared in manuscript.

Place	Date	Hour	Summary of Events and Information	Remarks and references to Appendices
Sheet 27 D.11.c.3.7.	1-2-18		Left billets at H camp for billets at D.8.c.7.7. Move complete 11 a.m.	
Sheet 27 D.8.c.7.7.	2-2-18		Training. One section at work erecting huts.	
"	3-2-18			
"	4-2-18		Training. One section erecting huts.	
"	5-2-18			
"	6-2-18			
"	7-2-18		Left billets for PROVEN station. entrained.	
"	8-2-18		Detrained at NOYON. proceeded to billets at VARESNES.	
(Sheet ST QUENTIN 18 VARESNES	9-2-18		Training.	
"	10-2-18		Training.	
"	11-2-18		H.2. of Coy moved to A.4.d.3.6. Sheet 70.D. N°1 sect – " 0.13.c.1.6. Sheet 66.C N°2 " 3 " T. 26.b.3.4. Sheet 66.C. N°4 " " G. 28.b.5.2 " 70.D. N°3 "	
Sheet 70.D. A.4.d.2.6.	12-2-18		Taking over work. Battle zone on the left & in front of Info front.	
	13-2-18		Worken battle zone + switch from VENDEUIL to LY-FONTAINE.	
	14-2-18			
	15-2-18			
	16-2-18			
	17-2-18			
	18-2-18			
	19-2-18			

WAR DIARY or INTELLIGENCE SUMMARY

Army Form C. 2118.

Sheet No 2

Place	Date	Hour	Summary of Events and Information	Remarks and references to Appendices
Hertford G.C. Huts 7° D. Aq.d.3.6.	25.2.18		Handed over work S. of Major OISE to 511 Fd by R.E. N.A. river OISE to T.4. central to 502 Fd by R.E. Proceeded with work in Battle Zone from T.4. central to N.16 central & on switch from VENDEUIL	
			G.L.N. FONTAINE	
			No 23. section & hy. H.Q. moved to M.36.d.7.9. Sheet 66.C.	
Sheet 66c M.36.d.7.9.	26.2.18		No 1 section on march. No 2 section in Battle Zone. No 3 section preparing bridges for demolition	
			between M.36. G.8.8 & T.3.C.8.1. No 4. section work on huts. 17th Platoon Buffs attached.	
	27.2.18		On 26th	
	28.2.18		On 27th. Orders to prepare to cover Battle Zone received 12 noon. Working parties cancelled & men recalled. Orders to man Battle Zone received 7.30 p.m. All men on platoon at FORT LIEZ	
			8.45 p.m. & immediately recalled	
			Casualties	
	2.2.18		Two other ranks joined as reinforcements from the R.E. Base Depot.	
	7.2.18		One " " " " " " " " " " " "	
	11.2.18		" " " " " No 5. Reinforcement by draft	
	17.2.18		Three " " " " " " the R.E. Base Depot.	
	19.2.18		Three " " " " " " "	
	28.2.18		Major R.L. Nunn R.E. left this Company to assume duties as A/Staff Captain C.E. XVIII Corps	
			Authority 5th Army Appointments dated 25-2-18.	

Wharb
O.C. 92nd Field Co R E
O.C. 92nd CAPTAIN E

18th Div.

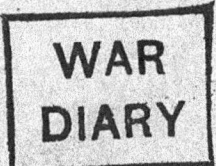

92nd FIELD COMPANY, R.E.

MARCH

1918

WAR DIARY or INTELLIGENCE SUMMARY

Army Form C. 2118

92nd Field Coy, R.E. 18

Vol. 1.

Place	Date	Hour	Summary of Events and Information	Remarks and references to Appendices
Shetgate SW. M.36.d.6.8.	1-3-18		No 1 Section at FORT VENDEUIL. N.18.c.5.5. with BUFFS & QUEENS attached platoon working on switch N.18.b. to N.10.d. No 2 + 4 Section at M.30.d.6.8 working on Battle zone N15 central to N.35 central. No 3 " preparing bridge on div. role over CROZAT canal for demolition. Also working on advanced enemy station M.36.d.4.2.	MM
	2-3-18 3-3-18 4-3-18 5-3-18 6-3-18		as 1-3-18	MM MM
	7-3-18		No 1 Section finish work on switch & work on line N.18.c. to N.36. central No 2 " bought one bridge to place over OISE nr O.26.c.7.9.	
	8-3-18 9-3-18 10-3-18		as 7-3-18	
	11-3-18		No 2 Section commenced putting bridge in position	MM
	12-3-18 13-3-18 14-3-18		as 11-3-18	
	15-3-18		Bridge finished. No 2 Section moves to N.28.b.6.8 & references work on line N.16.c. to N.36 central	MM
	16-3-18 17-3-18 18-3-18 19-3-18		as 15-3-18.	
	20-3-18		Warning prepare for attack received 5 p.m.	MM

Army Form C. 2118

WAR DIARY
or
INTELLIGENCE SUMMARY
(Erase heading not required.)

SHEET 2

Instructions regarding War Diaries and Intelligence Summaries are contained in F.S. Regs., Part II. and the Staff Manual respectively. Title Pages will be prepared in manuscript.

Place	Date	Hour	Summary of Events and Information	Remarks and references to Appendices
At ST QUENTIN SHEET.	21.3.18		2nd Pos & E. Savoy Platoon man Butte Jane 6.0 a.m. 3 Sects. standby to destroy bridges. No Relief. BUFFS & QUEEN'S Platoon on VENDEUIL FORT. Transport left MENESSIS 6 p.m. for COMMENCHON.	
	22.3.18.		No. 1 Pos & BUFF'S & QUEEN'S Platoon prematurely captured. No. 3 Section destroy all bridges between 6.15 & 6.50 a.m. after withdrawal of Brigade. 2.3. & 4 Pos & E. Savoy Platoon concentrate on ROUEZ, 11 a.m. Day in W. of NOUREUIL. Withdraw to ROUEZ 7 p.m.	
	23.3.18.		Day in W. of ROUEZ 10 a.m. Advanced & held high ground W. of NOUREUIL. Withdrew at nightfall over to Withdrawal of troops on flanks. No. 2 Sect. attached to comforts force dug in near FAUNY other Sects. alive thru COMMENCHON. Transport moved to MONDESCOURT. Breakfasted at CAILLOUEL & dug in W. of village & held line No.1 fect & No. 2 feet afven CAILLOUEL-CREPIGNY road. Transport moved to THIESCOURT (AMIENS sheet).	
	24.3.18		3 a.m. withdrew by order 55 Brig. & consolidated line to mile S.W. of CREPIGNY completed 6 a.m. Withdrew to BABŒUF thence to VARESNES arrived at latter 10.30 a.m. & collected inlying working parties. Under orders from G.O.C. 16 Div manned line S of R. OISE between VARESNES & BRETIGNY from 4 p.m. to dark (8 p.m.) then withdrew on KUTS. Transport to ESTRÉE ST DENIS	
	25.3.18		Moved to CAISNES then to MAMPCEL (SHEET 70 E. W.15 central).	
	26.3.18.		at " GRANGE des MOINS (SHEET 70 E. W.29 central).	
	27.3.18.		at " " " " "	
	28.3.18.		"	
	29.3.18		Move to MAMPCEL	
	30.3.18			
	31.3.18		Entrain at W.20. central at 3 a.m. Detrain at BOVES 6 p.m. (AMIENS SHEET).	

Army Form C. 2118

WAR DIARY
INTELLIGENCE SUMMARY SHEET. 3.
(Erase heading not required.)

Instructions regarding War Diaries and Intelligence Summaries are contained in F. S. Regs., Part II. and the Staff Manual respectively. Title Pages will be prepared in manuscript.

Place	Date	Hour	Summary of Events and Information	Remarks and references to Appendices
	4-3-18		2. O R s joined from Base Depot. (Reinforcements)	
	7-3-18		Major E.B. Alexander arrived from the 89th Field Coy R.E.	
	9-3-18		1. O R joined from Base Depot. (Reinforcement)	
	9-3-18		1 horse (rider) evacuated to M.V.S.	
	11-3-18		5. O R s joined Coy from Base Depot. SAVY. from boy.	
	12-3-18		1. O R wounded in action.	
	16-3-18		1. O R evacuated to C.C.S. (disease)	
	21-3-18		1. O R killed in action. 2. O R s wounded in action. II Lieut. C.K. Roylance R.E. and 2 9 O R s missing, believed prisoners of war.	
	23-3-18		4. O R s wounded in action, one of whom remains at duty.	
	29-3-18		Lieut. R. Weir R.E. posted to the 80th Field Coy R.E.	

[signature] Capt R.E.
for O.C. 92nd Field Company R.E.

18th Div.

92nd FIELD COMPANY, R.E.

A P R I L

1 9 1 8

WAR DIARY or INTELLIGENCE SUMMARY

Army Form C. 2118.

9.2 2nd Coy R.E.

Sheet N° 1   Vol 33

Place	Date	Hour	Summary of Events and Information	Remarks
4777E BOVES.	1-4-18		Dismounted at BOVES. Left BOVES 5 p.m. for T.11.a.9.5. sheet MONT LE VERVE.	
Sheet 62.D T.11.a.9.5	2-4-18		2 & 4 section shift T.11.a.9.5 2 p.m. for V.6.a.55. 55 from H.2. Transferred from there to 0.36.c.3.4. embarked on section of Sheet H.2a. N°3 section to GENTELLES.	
O.36.C.3.4.	3-4-18		2 & 4 sections further south on Sheet V.6. H.2a.	
	4-4-18	5 a.m	2 & 4 section billeted out of billets 5 mm 'gun moved to U.34.b.6.8. N°3 section heavily shelled in GENTELLE	
		5 a.m	N°3 section pull in & 200 yds arr. V.7.a.8.0 & V.7.a.6.3. N° 2 & 4 section move to T.11.a.9.5. necessary	
		2 p.m		
		7 p.m.	N°3 section withdraw with 75 field & move V.8.c.55 to V.8.c.9.5. return to HSC 11 p.m.	
BOVES.	5-4-18		Dismounted move to BOVES + 2 Lobes & 2 limber carts & water cart unused	
	6-4-18		"	
	7-4-18		Leave HSC 5.45 p.m + arrive 1300 yds in front of VILLERS BRETONNEUX. V.30.d.12.6 V.36.c.5.2	
	8-4-18		Relieve to HSC 5 a.m.	
	9-4-18		Dismounted dug ford E of LABAY V.3.C. central	
	10-4-18		" Transferred move to CRIEL	
	11-4-18		" LARUE ST PIERRE	
AMIENS	12-4-18		" move to ECOLE NORMALES des INSTITUTRICE AMIENS. Transferred to LA RUE ST PIERRE	
	13-4-18		Shot to livening. Transferred to LA HUSSOY. CONTY BEAUVAIS	
	14-4-18		"	
	15-4-18		"	
	16-4-18		"	

Army Form C. 2118.

WAR DIARY
or
INTELLIGENCE SUMMARY

Sheet N° 2.

(Erase heading not required.)

Instructions regarding War Diaries and Intelligence Summaries are contained in F. S. Regs, Part II. and the Staff Manual respectively. Title Pages will be prepared in manuscript.

Place	Date	Hour	Summary of Events and Information	Remarks and references to Appendices
AMIENS.	17.4.18		Training	
"	18.4.18			
"	19.4.18			
"	20.4.18			
"	21.4.18			
"	22.4.18			
"	23.4.18		Training. Reinforcements arrive & N°1 section reformed.	
"	24.4.18		Training.	
"	25.4.18			
"	26.4.18			
"	27.4.18			
"	28.4.18		Move to B.24.b.3.8. Officers reconoitre line	
"	29.4.18		Move to O.5.a.6.3.	
"	30.4.18		*Casualties*	
	1.4.18		1 Officer + 3 O.Rs wounded in action	
	4.4.18		3 O.Rs wounded in action	
	23.4.18		3 Officers and 60 O.R.s joined as reinforcements from R. E. Base Depot.	

for O. C. 92nd Field Coy R.E.

Army Form C. 2118.

WAR DIARY
or
INTELLIGENCE SUMMARY

(Erase heading not required.)

92 F.W. Coy, R.E.
May 1918.
Sheet No. 1.

Vol 34

Place	Date	Hour	Summary of Events and Information	Remarks and references to Appendices
C.5.a.6.3. Sheet 62.D.	1·5·18		Take over from 5th Australian Fd. Coy. Work on deep dugouts at D.18.d.0.5. two shelters over there dugouts D.24.a.1.7 D.23.b.7.1 D.18.d.75.15 D.17.c.6.2.	Mn
"	2·5·18 3·5·18	}	As above	
"	4·5·18		As 1·5·18. Also trench from D.24.b.5.5 to D.24 & 7·9 Sup. out.	
"	5·5·18		As 1·5·18.	
"	6·5·18		As 5·18 dugouts & Double Apron fence erected in front of LAVIEVILLE trench	
"	7·5·18		Dugouts continued D.11.c.4.4; D.17.a.5.5; D.16.b.4.3.	
"	8·5·18		" " Waterproof Bel. H.2 at P.9.b.3.7.	
"	9·5·18			
"	10·5·18			
"	11·5·18		Dugouts at D.18.d.0.5. D.24.a.1.7; D.21.b.7.1; assembled over to 79 Fd. Coy R.E. & other dugouts continued.	
"	12·5·18		Dugouts continued. 900' double Apron fence D.5.c.1.7.; D.11.a.4.8; D.11.a.8.5; D.11.a 4.0. gap in roads provided with knife rests.	
"	13·5·18		700' double Apron fence. D.11.d.5.5; D.17.a.4.5; D.17.a.1.5 Predon screen C.12.b.6.4. Pile shelters dugouts D15d.75.15 + D.17.c.6.2.	
"	14·5·18 16·5·18		Work on dry weather tracks around LAVIEVILLE. fence at C.11.a.6.4 finished 400 Y wire D.10d.70 to D16.b.4.4. Pile shelters dugouts. Dry weather tracks. forts at D.16.d.15.85; D.16.d.7.2; D.23.a.2.85; D.23.a.2.6	
"	17·5·18		130' C.T. to average depth 2'. Dry weather Ry. trucks. forts completed. 500' Double Apron fence. D.22.a.5.0 to D.22.A.9.0.	

Army Form C. 2118.

WAR DIARY
or
INTELLIGENCE SUMMARY
(Erase heading not required.)

Reel No 2.

Instructions regarding War Diaries and Intelligence Summaries are contained in F. S. Regs., Part II. and the Staff Manual respectively. Title Pages will be prepared in manuscript.

Place	Date	Hour	Summary of Events and Information	Remarks and references to Appendices
C.3.a.6.3 Mult 62.D.	18.5.18		1200' x screen erected between B.16.b.4.8 & D.17.b.5.7 ALBERT-AMIENS road.	
	19.5.18		Deperication hedges continued. LAVIEVILLE C.T. & ford at D.23.a.7.2 commenced.	
	20.5.18		Three tracks completed. Bomb proof dugout for horse lines.	
	21.5.18		Marout at D.15.c.3.0. on dry weather track. LAVIEVILLE C.T. & ford	
	22.5.18		Both out D.ID. work'ed commenced.	
	23.5.18		Overground tracks finished. C.T. & fords continued.	
			Bridges + C.T. continued.	
			1000' x double apron wire D.22.a.7.0 to D.16.d.2.5	
	24.5.18		C.T. completed.	
	25.5.18		Demolition work to 17.Div. & lock over work on BAZIEUX line & O.P. at mill D.10.7.1	
	26.5.18		Work on Begieux line & mill	
	27.5.18		" "	
	28.5.18		" "	
	29.5.18		" "	
	30.5.18		" Took over from 503rd (Wessex) Fd. Coy. R.E. Relieving hills.	
	31.5.18			

Army Form C. 2118.

WAR DIARY
or
INTELLIGENCE SUMMARY
(Erase heading not required.)

Sheet No 3

Instructions regarding War Diaries and Intelligence Summaries are contained in F. S. Regs., Part II. and the Staff Manual respectively. Title Pages will be prepared in manuscript.

Place	Date	Hour	Summary of Events and Information	Remarks and references to Appendices
			Casualties	
	2-5-18		II Cpl. (con mind) to Sappers and Transferred to 30th Field C.R.E.	
	1-5-18		1 O.R. Transferred to 12th Div. H.Q	
	8-5-18		1 O.R. admitted to Hospital and remained same day	
	9-5-18		1 Horse (Rider) destroyed	
	15-5-18		2 Horses (Rider & L.D) evacuated to 30th M.V.S.	
	18-5-18		1 O.R. wounded by Shell fire	
	19-5-18		1 O.R. wounded sick	
	19-5-18		1 Horse (Rider) killed by Shell fire	
	18-5-18		1 L.D. Horse arrived as reinforcement	
	28-5-18		1 Horse (Rider) evacuated to 30th M.V.S.	

[signature] Capt. R.E.
for O.C. 92nd Field Co R.E.

WAR DIARY or INTELLIGENCE SUMMARY

Army Form C. 2118.

92nd Bn. CEF

Sheet No. 1

June 1918

Vol 35

Place	Date	Hour	Summary of Events and Information	Remarks and references to Appendices
C.5.c.8.7. Sheet 62.D.	1.6.18.		Reconnoitring trench M.2.5 for tack overlay of Bn. Hqrs. & Support Battalion H.2 V.29.b.9.7.	Referred to in 2 copies SENLIS Sheet
	2.6.18.		As 1.6.18. In addition recon. in front of own trench.	
	3.6.18.		Brisbane Support, Australia trench & Melbourne trench deepened. Nelson & Bath H.2.d. created.	
	4.6.18.		As 3.6.18.	
	5.6.18.		As 3.6.18. In addition wiring of 5 yds. S of Australia & recon on Murray strong point V.30.a.9.7 & V.30.b.5.7	
	6.6.18.		As 5.6.18.	
	7.6.18.		As 6.6.18.	
	8.6.18.		Brigade relief (no such done).	
	9.6.18.		Work on Murray strong point	
	10.6.18.		" " " " "	
	11.6.18.		" " " today. No enemy to interfere. No night watch enemy to interfere from B.G.C. 53 Left Principle	
	12.6.18.		As 11.6.18.	
	13.6.18.		Work on Murray & Melbourne strong points & also trench system V.30.a.6.5 & wire W.25.a.5.2 & W.26.a.1.7.	
	14.6.18.		Work on Murray. No night watch owing to operations	
	15.6.18.		" " & Melbourne strong point G. Wiring J.W.25.c.8.3.6. W.26.a.4.9.	
	16.6.18.		" " " & wiring the latter	
	17.6.18.		As 17.6.18.	
	18.6.18.		As 17.6.18. Also erecting trenches shelters & covering 200 yds HENENCOURT-SENLIS road	
	19.6.17.		Brigade Relief (no such done)	
	20.6.18.		Work on MURRAY & MELBOURNE Strong Points, wiring MELBOURNE TRENCH, covering	
	21.6.18.		HENENCOURT-SENLIS Road, completed.	
	22.6.18.		As for 21.6.18.	

WAR DIARY or **INTELLIGENCE SUMMARY**

Army Form C. 2118.

Sheet N° 2

Place	Date	Hour	Summary of Events and Information	Remarks and references to Appendices
C5c 87	23.6.18		as for 22.6.18	
Sh 62.D	24.6.18		as for 23.6.18	
	25.6.18		as for 24.6.18	
	26.6.18		Perfect relief. (No incidents) Coy relieved by 50th Field Coy RE and took over work of 79th Field Coy RE in Divisional Reserve.	A.I
	27.6.18		Work on bomb stops in JAKETS TR & JAKETS SUPP, New C.T. in CAVALRY SWITCH, Tramways etc in HAM Redoubt.	A.II
	28.6.18		also 2 Battalion Infantry (7th Queen's & Pt.Bn/Surreys)	
	29.6.18		Work as for 28.6.18. Also 2 Battalion Infantry working on widening HENENCOURT System.	A.III
	30.6.18		Work as for 29.6.18 except 2 Coys Infantry who	

CASUALTIES

4.6.18		II Lieut. G. Harley R.E. wounded in action		
16.6.18		II Lieut. R.D. Acraman R.E. joined as reinforcement. 5-6-18.		
18.6.18		1 Horse (Rider) and 1 Mule arrived		
16.6.18		1 O.R. Killed in action		
20.6.18		II Lieut. F.J. Thisen R.E. joined as reinforcement from Base.		
21.6.18		1 O.R. joined as reinforcement from Base.		
22.6.18		1 O.R. transferred to 180th Tunnelling Co. R.E.		

Palmer
Major R.E.
Comdg 92nd (Fd.) Co. R.E.

Army Form C. 2118.

WAR DIARY
or
INTELLIGENCE SUMMARY

(Erase heading not required.)

92nd Field Coy (3rd Army?) Vol 36

Instructions regarding War Diaries and Intelligence Summaries are contained in F.S. Regs., Part II. and the Staff Manual respectively. Title Pages will be prepared in manuscript.

July 1918

Place	Date	Hour	Summary of Events and Information	Remarks and references to Appendices
C.S.C.8.8.	1.7.18		Work on tramlines V.22.6.33. V22.6.8.8. V226.7.1. & Ham Rept. Also reconnaissance of V.22.6.4.7 & general	
SENLIS (Special Hut)	2.7.18		work on trestles on HENENCOURT system.	
	3.7.18		As 1.7.18	
	4.7.18		As 1.7.18 (2) Rest camp completed.	
	5.7.18		Working MELBOURNE C.T.	
	6.7.18		"	
	7.7.18		As 3.7.18. Also work on POSSUM & new trench C.T. in V.22.b. connecting TERRACE & CAVALRY.	
	8.7.18		As 7.7.18.	
	9.7.18		Wiring round HAM COPSE. All troops employed. Little alteration from 9.P.M. to 3 a.m.	
	10.7.18		As 7.7.18. Also 550 yds wire round HAM COPSE.	
	11.7.18		As 10.7.18 also branch line over to 517 Fld Coy R.E. Infantry platoons upon Battalions	
	12.7.18		"	
AMIENS MAP. 17.	13.7.18 4.a.m.		Coy entrained at CONTAY. Transport proceeded by road. Infantry debussed PREVIGNY & marched to LA CHAUSSEE.	
	14.7.18		Training & repairs including training of L.G. team for Lewis & 2 air rifles per section etc.	
	15-29.7.18		2 days pontooning	
			Coy embus at LACHAUSSEE debus at PONT NOYELLES & proceeds to I.5.d.9.8. Transport proceeds	
Mad 62 D	30.7.18		by road, same flat. Take over from 15th Aus. Fd. Coy.	
			Montieres & Trestle dump at VILLERS BOCAGE. No. 1 section moves to J.9.6.8.6.	
	31.7.18			J.10.h.5.3
			No. 2 " " J.9.b.8.6	
			Infantry platoons return	

JMK

Army Form C. 2118.

WAR DIARY
or
INTELLIGENCE SUMMARY

(Erase heading not required.)

Sheet No 2

Place	Date	Hour	Summary of Events and Information	Remarks and references to Appendices
			Casualties	
	6-7-18		1 L.D. Horse evacuated to 30th M.V.S.	
	5-7-18		1 N.C.O. transferred to Horse Establishment as instructor	
	7-7-18		2 O.R. evacuated Sick	
	15-7-18		1 L.D. Horse evacuated to 30th M.V.S.	
	16-7-18		1 N.C.O. transferred to Cadet Distribution Centre, R.A.F. LONDON.	
	15-7-18		1 O.R. evacuated Sick "	
	23-7-18		1 O/R "	
	26-7-18		1 O.R. transferred to Cadet Distribution Centre, R.A.F. LONDON	

Major R.E.
for O.C. 92nd Field Coy R.E.

18th Division
ENGINEERS

92nd FIELD COMPANY, R. E.

AUGUST, 1918.

C.R.E. 18th Division.

Certified the attached is a true copy of the War Diary for the month of August.

W. Hoyland 2/Lieut R.E.
for, O.C. 92nd Field Company R.E.

Forwarded, as requested,

[signature] Lieutenant
for C.R.E. 18th Div.

WAR DIARY
or
INTELLIGENCE SUMMARY.
(Erase heading not required.)

Army Form C. 2118.

92nd Field Company R.E. BEF No.1.

Vol 38

Instructions regarding War Diaries and Intelligence Summaries are contained in F.S. Regs., Part II. and the Staff Manual respectively. Title pages will be prepared in manuscript.

Place	Date	Hour	Summary of Events and Information	Remarks and references to Appendices
Bluet 62d	1-8-18		Coy working on forward communications	
I.5.d.9.8	2-8-18		Wiring KOBAR C.T. at K.13.a.6.8. Dugout at J.4.d.5.8.	
"	3-8-18		As 2-8-18.	
"	4-8-18		Our Bow H.Q. at J.18.d.3.8. Making & casting concretors ready for forward use.	
"	5-8-18		"	
"	6-8-18		Enemy attack prevented completion of Jobs. Several casualties in No.2 Section	
"	7-8-18		Old Bow H.Q. comp &c.	
"	8-8-18		No. 1 Section were placing points directly ground is held along BRAY-CORBIE sunken road. No. 3 Section dug line in K.30. & following road to SAILLY LAURETTE. No. 2 Section wire line in K.14.c.	
"	9-8-18		Coy ... line from K.14.c.6.1. to K.14.d.9.4.	
Senlis, Special Bluet	10-8-18		Coy move to C.S.C.5.8.	
V.27.6.5.1	11-8-18		Coy ... to HENENCOURT Chateau V.27.6.5.1.	
"	12-8-18		HENENCOURT defences & accommodation	
"	13-8-18		" & roads in V.28.c.	
"	14-8-18		As 13-8-18	
"	15-8-18		Road HENENCOURT—MILLENCOURT to V.26.a.9.3 made usable for heavy artillery.	
"	16-8-18		Kept in repair. Work on HENENCOURT defences.	
"	17-8-18		Do 16-8-18.	

Army Form C. 2118.

WAR DIARY
or
INTELLIGENCE SUMMARY.
(Erase heading not required.)

Sheet 2

92nd F.

Instructions regarding War Diaries and Intelligence Summaries are contained in F. S. Regs. Part II and the Staff Manual respectively. Title pages will be prepared in manuscript.

Place	Date	Hour	Summary of Events and Information	Remarks and references to Appendices
Senlis Bivouac	18.8.18		Work on HEMENCOURT - ALBERT road. Overland tracks: E.3.c.4.4. to W.27.c.1.2. & D.4.d.2.2. to D.6.a.8.3. Also W.21.a.9.0.	
Sheet V.27. & 51.	19.8.18			
	20.8.18		- also overland tracks: W.21.a.8.0. to W.22.a.2.5, & E.3.a.3.6. to E.3.d.2.4. & E.3.d.2.7. to E.3.d.7.2.	
	21.8.18		Rest.	
BECOURT. Sheet	22.8.18	7 a.m.	Infantry Bridges thrown over Ancre at E.H.a.5.1, E.H.c.5.9, E.H.c.5.7, & E.H.c.5.6 in time for first Infantry wave to cross road made passable from E.3.d.23 to E.H.c.5.9 by No 4 Section	
		9 a.m.	Trestle Bridge complete over river ANCRE at E.H.c.5.9. by No 1 Section. Section carries on clearing roads.	
		2 p.m.	Trestle Bridge ready for traffic at W.28.c.4.4. Road from MILLENCOURT to W.29.c.4.4.8 on to W.28.c.7.6. & W.28.d.5.4.8 forward towards LA-BOISSELLE cleared for light traffic by No 2 Section.	
			No 3 Section proceeded with BUFFS through ALBERT to make strong points but were not required, returning to camp 10.0 pm. During the day 6 contact mines & many booby trapped trembles, several strong points at E.1.a.2.8 & E.H.c.6.6. developed. Bridges repaired. Canvas tanks at W.29.c.7.8. made and filled.	
	23.8.18		Springs at E.1.a.2.8 & E.H.c.6.6. developed. Bridges repaired. Canvas tanks at W.29.c.7.8. made and filled.	
	24.8.18		Roads and approaches made to Springs as above. Bridges repaired.	

Army Form C. 2118.

WAR DIARY
or
INTELLIGENCE SUMMARY. Sheet 23

(Erase heading not required.)

Place	Date	Hour	Summary of Events and Information	Remarks and references to Appendices
V.27.t.5.1.	25.8.18		No 1, 2 & 3 Sections move to X.26.d.3.2. just S. of BECOURT Chateau. No 3 Section attached to BUFFS, as advance guard. Work on roads.	
BECOURT Sheet.	26.8.18		BUFFS & QUEENS Platoons come up to 1 & 2 Sections. Remainder of Coy move up to E.10.b.2.8. Work on roads etc. also well & canvas tanks at X.29.8.8.3.	2 in FRICOURT & BOTTOM WOOD
	27.8.18 28.8.18 29.8.18		Do 27.8.18 " 28.8.18	
ALBERT Sheet. Contd	30.8.18		1, 2 & 3 Sections move with Platoons to B.29.c.7.2. erect Bus advance H.Q. at same Rept. Coy do not occupy their H.Q. hut 35 t Bde do. Further this H.D. worked on at S.27.a.2.6.	
	31.8.18		Three Sns etc move to X.30.a.8.9. Work on Adv Div H.Q. at S.27.a.26. & Bde H.Q. at B.2.a.0.6.	
			Casualties	
	1.8.18		1. O.R. killed in action	
	6.8.18		2/Lt BAYLEY RE and 6 ORs wounded in action	
	8.8.18		2/Lt HALL RE killed in action. 2/Lt MEEH RE and 1 O.R. wounded in action.	
	13.8.18		2/Lts HOYLAND, DAVIES & THOMAS, joined Coy from R.E. Base.	
	15.8.18		6 ORs joined from R.E. Base Depot (reinforcements)	
	22.8.18		3 ORs killed in action. 2/Lt DAVIES & 8 ORs wounded in action	
	26.8.18		2 ORs joined from R.E. Base Depot (reinforcements.)	

Sgn/Lt H. O. James Capt RE
for OC 172 Field Co RE

WAR DIARY or INTELLIGENCE SUMMARY

Army Form C. 2118.

92 Fd Coy RE

Sept 1918

Vol. 39

Place	Date	Hour	Summary of Events and Information	Remarks and references to Appendices
D.24.a.4.2 R.W.62.c.	21.9.18		Disposition of Coy. on 20.9.18. Work in progress H.2 & Enemy situation in RONSSOY	
	22.9.18		At 21.9.18. also with an armoured trench. E.16.6.2.3 to RONSSOY	
	23.9.18		At 22.9.18.	
	24.9.18		Handed over work formerly held by B.Coy 37 Div. U.S.A. army Coy concentrate at D.24.a.4.2 R.E. Materials upon Brigade. Sights carried by No.3 Section 400 yds E of Duncan Post.	
D.4.c.3.9.	25.9.18 26.9.18		Coy move to D.4.c.3.9. & attached on 54 Bde. H.Q.	
	27.9.18 28.9.18		At 25.9.18. Conclusive recce at D.4.c.3.9. Coy move to E.4 central & are joined by platoon. Sections move from Villers to EPEHY ready to bridge canal in VENDHUILE unable to proceed as infantry do not occupy the village.	
	29.9.18 30.9.18		Sections move from Villers to TOMBOIS FARM. No work possible. Reconnaissance of bridge & canal. & Lt. Martel under heavy M.G. fire.	

Army Form C. 2118.

WAR DIARY
or
INTELLIGENCE SUMMARY

(Erase heading not required.)

SHEET 3

Instructions regarding War Diaries and Intelligence Summaries are contained in F. S. Regs., Part II. and the Staff Manual respectively. Title Pages will be prepared in manuscript.

Place	Date	Hour	Summary of Events and Information	Remarks and references to Appendices
			Casualties	
	6.9.18		"Lieut E Crozier R.E. & 22 OR's joined as reinforcements from Base Depot	
	9.9.18		1 N.C.O. transferred to Base.	
	9.9.18		1 Horse (riding) Evacuated to 20th M.V.S.	
	16.9.18		Major E.A.Alexander wounded in action (gassed).	
	19.9.18		1 OR. Wounded in action.	
	23.9.18		1 OR " " "	
	23.9.18		1 OR " " "	
	25.9.18		2 OR's " " "	

[signature] Major R.E.
O.C. 92nd Field Coy. R.E.

Army Form C. 2118.

WAR DIARY
or
INTELLIGENCE SUMMARY

(Erase heading not required.)

92nd / 1st /161 Coy R.E Sheet 1.

September 1918

Place	Date	Hour	Summary of Events and Information	Remarks and references to Appendices
ALBERT continued S.29.c.8.3	1.9.18.		No 1 section on wells & reconnaissance E of COMBLES. No 2 section on COMBLES-SAILLY road. No 3 section on COMBLES-RANCOURT road. All sections started from camp at 3.30 a.m. 2 v 3 sections return to B.4.a.29.	7/1
B.4.a.29.	2.9.18.		Whole Coy moves from X.30.a.8.3 to B.4.a.29, which whole Coy unreadable. Work on new Bry H.2 at Bazentin & cookhouse.	2/1
"	3.9.18.		Made a 2.9.18. TRONES WOOD to FRENICOURT. One section attached to QUEENS as vanguard. Reconnaissance by Lt Thomas R.E of CANAL du NORD. On repairing Rly West D.1 (57.C.5.W.)	3/1
"	4.9.18		Work as 3.9.18.	4/1
S.29.b.4.4	5.9.18.		By move to S.28.b.4.4. Cableway. Battery for Brigade etc. Footbridge field for Brigade. Rec'd armament at TRONES WOOD S.30.c.1.S.	5/1
"	6.9.18		"	6/1
"	7.9.18		"	
"	8.9.18			
"	9.9.18			
"	10.9.18			
"	11.9.18			
"	12.9.18		As 6.9.18	
"	13.9.18		No 1 section move to LIERAMONT. Pull'g 2 Oj NE other below as 6.9.18. No 2 section on new Bty H.2.	7/1
"	14.9.18		No 2.	Brigade
Sheltezen D.24.a.42.	15.9.18		Remainder of Coy less No 2 section move to D.24.a.42. Net work on armament. Accommodation for Coy on Bry H.2. No 2 section repels dummy Lewis at F.13.d.4.1.	8/1
"	16.9.18		2 sections attached to troops at B.4. ex. 1.H.2. B.H.2. 1 section moves forward to F.21.b.5.3 + makes new path of Brigade H.2	9/1
"	17.9.18		No section returns completely. Our armament of TRONES WOOD. No 2 section removed at F.21.b.5.3 works on Brigade 1 Battalion H.22	
"	18.9.18		No 1 + 3 sections with attached platoon move to E.23.b.5.9.	
"	19.9.18		No 2 section move to E.23.b.5.9. All sections on accommodation except No 4 on water supply at LIERAMONT + AIZECOURT LE BAS	10/1

D/713.

C.R.E. 18th Division.

Herewith War Diary for the month of October.

W. Royland II Lieut R.E.
for, O.C. 92nd Field Coy R.E.

1st November '18

WAR DIARY
or
INTELLIGENCE SUMMARY.

(Erase heading not required.)

Army Form C. 2118.

92ND FLD COY R.E.
Sheet 1.
Vol 39

Place	Date	Hour	Summary of Events and Information	Remarks and references to Appendices
NURLU Pt 63.9 Ref 62.C	1-10-18		Coy concentrated at NURLU.	
	2-10-18		Transport moves to CONTAY, afresh, infantry to COMBLES. By move by bus to CONTAY, guns & transport there. (LENS Sheet)	
CONTAY	3-10-18 to 15-10-18		Reat & training. Officially fortening, unfrowling & evacuation in field work also inspection & tenes jumps.	
	16-10-18		Transfor of cars for MAMETZ.	
	17-10-18		By entrained at HEILLY detrained at ROISEL, march transport at TEMPLE VX LA FOSSE. (S.T. QUENTIN SHEET) Move to BEAUREVOIR. B. march route ELINCOURT.	
	18-10-18 19-10-18		Rest.	
ELINCOURT (S.T. QUENTIN SHEET)	20-10-18 21-10-18 22-10-18		To MAUROIS. Remain at MAUROIS. By move to LE CATEAU. T work on telephone wires under at wood junction on BOUSIES Rd. L.4. c.5.9	
LE CATEAU K.35.031 (W.15) B.M.E.	23-10-18 24-10-18 25-10-18 26-10-18		March as 23.10.18. Cullin infantry trucks L.5. a.4.6. F30.c.3.4. F29.a.4.7.6. F24.c.7.1	

Army Form C. 2118.

WAR DIARY
or
INTELLIGENCE SUMMARY.

(Erase heading not required.)

9² 4th/by R.E. Sheet 2

Instructions regarding War Diaries and Intelligence Summaries are contained in F. S. Regs., Part II. and the Staff Manual respectively. Title pages will be prepared in manuscript.

Place	Date	Hour	Summary of Events and Information	Remarks and references to Appendices
LE CATEAU K.35.d.3.1 (Sheet 5.7.B. NE.)	27.10.18		On 27.10.18	
	28.10.18		Border hostile shell D.H.Q. LE CATEAU. Gas Mustard on road BUSIGNIES. Prisoners patrol road at K.25.b.3.1.	
	29.10.18		Artillery hostile K.30 central. Yard H.D.4.2. Gas violent & refugees at Busigny Batt H.20 on BUSIGNIES & Artillery hostile H.20	
	30.10.18		Hostile track F.22.b.2.0 K.15.c.7.b. Worked Dec H.? to H.2. Sore hair over to K.34.c.5.4.	
K.34.C.5.4.	31.10.18		Work at Box H.2 Gas violent on & near BUSIGNIES	

Army Form C. 2118.

WAR DIARY
or
INTELLIGENCE SUMMARY.
(Erase heading not required.)

Instructions regarding War Diaries and Intelligence Summaries are contained in F. S. Regs., Part II. and the Staff Manual respectively. Title pages will be prepared in manuscript.

Place	Date	Hour	Summary of Events and Information	Remarks and references to Appendices
			CASUALTIES.	
	5-10-18		Capt J.C.B. Davies appointed to Command of 92nd Field Coy RE, vice Major E.B. Alexander. M.C. RE (quoted per A.G.S No A.9 55/4879 (0) dated 25-9-18	
	5-10-18		2 ORs admitted to hospital, gassed.	
	6-10-18		4 ORs reinforcement arrived from RE Base Depot	
	7-10-18		II Lieut R.S. Alexander proceeded to RE Training School, Rouen. II Lieut J.Z. Davies M.C. RE joined from RE Base Depot	
	8-10-18		Lieut H.E. Wise D.M.C.H. posted to 79th Field Coy RE	
	13-10-18		3 ORs reinforcement arrived from RE Base Depot	
	19-10-18		1 OR home destroyed (broken leg)	
	25-10-18		1 OR reinforcement arrived from RE Base Depot. I Lieut G. Chandler killed in action	
	25-10-18		Major J.C.B. Davies RE wounded in action, remains at duty.	
	25-10-18		1 OR home evacuated to 30 M.V.S.	
	25-10-18		Major J.C.B. Davies RE awarded the Military Cross as C.R.O. 46.1 dated Feb 15.10.18	
	27-10-18		2 men arrived from 1st Army A.S.C.	

Major RE.
R.E. 92nd Field Coy RE.

WAR DIARY or INTELLIGENCE SUMMARY

Army Form C. 2118.

922nd F.A.Coy R.E.
Nov 1918
Sheet 1.

Place	Date	Hour	Summary of Events and Information	Remarks and references to Appendices
K34.c.5.4.	1/11/18		Sec. carrying on BOUSSIES (Mahin) roles trench flares roads to LE CATEAU (Mahin) + M.G. Loads. Quarry work	M
Subs 7 B.N.E.	2/11/18			
	3/11/18		do. do.	M
	4/11/18			
F2 & L7.4	5/11/18		Left camp at 12 P & C 7.4. Work on priyards Rd. 11.52a. Rapprochement march on FOREST de MORMAL + 3 m-mi S. chargeforn	M
Subs 7B.N.E.			close 5 m ROUTE de PREUX from A17.d.6.6 to B.8.c.7.9 + 6 chayn from autorisin.	
			ROUTE de FONTAINE between A23.d.3.1 & B.12.d.4.8. (Shek 57 A.N.W.)	
	6/11/18		274 Felima moves to L.3.c.9.4 + work on bridge L.8.c.9.2 (….)	
	7/11/18		Two Felima clearing road at L.8.c.9.2. & then actions on road in FOREST de MORMAL	M
L.3.c.9.4	8/11/18		by move to C.8.c.9.4. Clearing road at C.13.d.5.5.	
Sheet 57.A.N.W.	9/11/18		Thed. employed build on C.14.15 + 9. to LEVAL + in bridges C.18.c.5.5 & C.19.c.8.3	M
	10/11/18		by move to LEVAL. Work on 9.11.18.	
C.10.d.6.6	11/11/18		Work on 9/11/18. Armistice commenced 11.00.	
	12/11/18			
	13/11/18		Work on bridges C.10.c.5.5 + C.18.a.2.1.	
	14/11/18		Two sections work on bridge C.18.a.2.1 + two clearing debris to lower ford at C.19.a.30	
	15/11/18			
	16/11/18		to do. 16/11/18.	
	17/11/18			

Army Form C. 2118.

WAR DIARY
or
INTELLIGENCE SUMMARY.

92 FLD COY R.E.
Nov 1918.
Sheet 2

(Erase heading not required.)

Instructions regarding War Diaries and Intelligence Summaries are contained in F. S. Regs., Part II. and the Staff Manual respectively. Title pages will be prepared in manuscript.

Place	Date	Hour	Summary of Events and Information	Remarks and references to Appendices
MAUROIS	19/11/18		Coy move to MAUROIS	
Sheet 57.B. U.3.a.9.6.	20/11/18		Coy move to BELINCOURT	
	21/11/18			
	22/11/18		Company billets in BELINCOURT. Refloring Droels & pavements locally confusing	
	23/11/18			
	24/11/18			
	25/11/18			
	26/11/18			
	27/11/18			
	28/11/18		Practice Divisional Inspection	
	29/11/18			
	30/11/18		Ian 21/11/18.	

Army Form C. 2118.

WAR DIARY
or
INTELLIGENCE SUMMARY

(Erase heading not required.) Sheet 3.

Place	Date	Hour	Summary of Events and Information	Remarks and references to Appendices
			CASUALTIES.	
	2-11-18		1 O.R. admitted to hospital	
	3-11-18		2 O.Rs " "	
	8-11-18		3 O.Rs Joined Coy as reinforcements from R.E. Base Depot	
	3-11-18		1 L.D. horses arrived from 30th M.V.S.	
	3-11-18		2nd Lieut J.L. Davies R.E. awarded M.C. auth. A.R.O. 1605.	
	5-11-18		1 O.R. reported from hospital	
	7-11-18		1 O.R. admitted to "	
	8-11-18		1 O.R. " "	
	9-11-18		1 O.R. reported from "	
	11-11-18		4 C.S.M Gaffan 83rd R.A Mule found from R.E. Base Depot (Reinforcement).	
	15-11-18		1 O.R. discharged (Brogan G.)	
	17-11-18		1 O.R. admitted to hospital	
	19-11-18		1 Riv. + 2 L.D. Horses arrived from 30th M.V.S.	
	20-11-18		1 Rider arrive from 80th Field Coy R.E.	
	20-11-18		1 O.R. admitted to hospital	
	23-11-18		1 L.D. Horse Evacuated to 30th M.V.S. (debility)	
	26-11-18		2 L.D. Horses land admitted to hospital	
	29-11-18		1 Rider Evacuated to 30th M.V.S. (General enlargement).	

[signature]
Major R.E.
O.C. 92nd Field Coy R.E.

WAR DIARY or INTELLIGENCE SUMMARY

Army Form C. 2118.

9 (2nd/1st Ed. Pty.) R.E.
December 1918.

Place	Date	Hour	Summary of Events and Information	Remarks and references to Appendices
ELINCOURT Sheet 57B U3a9b	1.12.18		Church Parade	
	2.12.18		Divisional Review	
	3.12.18		Repairing houses in ELINCOURT, and demolition of dumps & grenades located by air-fary dits.; Rwg mailed the Division, company marking G-STRAIN	
	4.12.18		ditto	
	5.12.18		ditto	
	6.12.18		ditto	
	7.12.18		ditto	
	8.12.18		Church parade	
	9.12.18		As on 3.12.18	
	10.12.18		"	
	11.12.18		"	
	12.12.18		Repairing houses in MALINCOURT and VILLERS OUTREAUX; demolition of dumps located by air-fary	
	13.12.18		"	
	14.12.18		"	
	15.12.18		Church parade	
VILLERS OUTRÉAUX Sheet 57B T.15 central	16.12.18		Company moved to VILLERS OUTRÉAUX	
	17.12.18		As on 12.12.18	
	18.12.18		"	
	19.12.18		"	
	20.12.18		"	
	21.12.18		"	
	22.12.18		Church parade	
	23.12.18		As on 12.12.18	
	24.12.18		"	
	25.12.18		Xmas break	
	26.12.18		"	
	27.12.18		"	
	28.12.18		"	
	29.12.18		Church parade	
	30.12.18		As on 12.12.18	
	31.12.18		"	

Army Form C. 2118.

WAR DIARY
INTELLIGENCE SUMMARY.

92nd Field Coy. R.E.

December 1918.

SHEET 2.

(Erase heading not required.)

Instructions regarding War Diaries and Intelligence Summaries are contained in F. S. Regs., Part II. and the Staff Manual respectively. Title pages will be prepared in manuscript.

Place	Date	Hour	Summary of Events and Information	Remarks and references to Appendices
			Casualties	
	7-12-18		5 O.Rs joined Coy from R.E. Base Depot (reinforcements)	
	12-12-18		2 O.Rs admitted to hospital	
	13-12-18		1 O.R. reported from hospital	
	14-12-18		1 " " " "	
	17-12-18		2 O.Rs joined Coy from R.E. Base Depot (reinforcements)	
	"		2nd Lt R.A. Fitzroy RE joined Coy from Base	
	23/12		1 L/D. Horse received from 30th M.V.S	
	25/12		1 O.R. reported from hospital	
	26/12		1 L/D. Horse casualties to 30th M.V.S	
	30/12		1 O.R. admitted to hospital	

O.C. 92nd (Fd.) Co. R.E.

WAR DIARY Sheet 1
or
INTELLIGENCE SUMMARY

Army Form C. 2118.

92nd Field Company R.E.
January 1919

Place	Date	Hour	Summary of Events and Information	Remarks and references to Appendices
Sh.57.B. T.15 & 21.9	1.1.19 to 17.1.19		by at VILLERS OUTRÉAUX. Work repairing billets etc. & destroying dumps shells & grenades in axe were T.M. N+5.	
	18.1.19		H.2 & 2 sections moved to J.22 central remainder of by remain at T.15d.1.9.	
J.22 central	19.1.19 20.1.19		2 sections finishing work commd T.15d.1.9 INCHY 2 sections commd	
	21.1.19		2 sections moved to H.2 from T.15 at 11.9	
	22.1.19 to 31.1.19		by engaged repairing houses etc & destroying dumps shells & grenades in area around INCHY.	

Army Form C. 2118.

WAR DIARY Sheet 2
or
INTELLIGENCE SUMMARY. 92nd Field Coy RE
January 1919

(Erase heading not required.)

Instructions regarding War Diaries and Intelligence Summaries are contained in F. S. Regs, Part II. and the Staff Manual respectively. Title pages will be prepared in manuscript.

Place	Date	Hour	Summary of Events and Information	Remarks and references to Appendices
			Casualties	
	2/1/19		1 OR admitted to hospital	
	5/1/19		3 OR's joined Coy from RE Base Depot. (Reinforcements)	
	6/1/19		1 OR proceeded to England for demobilisation	
	7/1/19		3 OR's " " " "	
	11/1/19		4 OR's joined Coy from RE Base Depot (Reinforcements)	
	12/1/19		1 L.D. Mule drawn from 30th M.V.S.	
	12/1/19		2 OR's proceeded to England for demobilisation	
	14/1/19		3 " Riders drawn from 30th M.V.S.	
			1 OR proceeded to England for demobilisation	
	17/1/19		1 OR " " " "	
	18/1/19		2 nd Lt. R.J. Milne left Coy for RE School E.L. Gosport.	
	19/1/19		4 OR's to England for demobilisation	
	20/1/19		1 Rider & 1 L.D. horse drawn from 30th M.V.S.	
	20/1/19		4 OR's proceeded to England for demobilisation	
	21/1/19		3 Riders evacuated to 30th M.V.S.	
	22/1/19		3 OR's proceeded to England for demobilisation	
	24/1/19		2 " " " "	
	25/1/19		2 " " " "	
	26/1/19		2 " " " "	
	27/1/19		2 " " " "	
	31/1/19			

[signed] Major RE
OC. 92nd Field Coy RE

Army Form C. 2118.

WAR DIARY
or
INTELLIGENCE SUMMARY.

Sheet No. 1
92nd Field Coy R.E.
February 1919 Vol 4 3

(Erase heading not required.)

Instructions regarding War Diaries and Intelligence Summaries are contained in F. S. Regs. Part II. and the Staff Manual respectively. Title pages will be prepared in manuscript.

Place	Date	Hour	Summary of Events and Information	Remarks and references to Appendices
Sheet 57 B	1.2.19 to 14.2.19		Coy engaged repairing billets for brigade & destruction of this stables & tombs etc	
Iswaded	15.2.19		Coy move to CAUDRY. Issue 7.2	
Issue 7.2	16.2.19 to 28.2.19		Coy engaged repairing billets etc for 55 Inf brigade & destruction of hand artillery etc	

Army Form C. 2118.

WAR DIARY
or
INTELLIGENCE SUMMARY.
(Erase heading not required.)

Sw.53. 92nd Field Company R.E.
February 1919

Place	Date	Hour	Summary of Events and Information	Remarks and references to Appendices
18th Div.	1/2/19		Casualties	
	1/2/19		6 ORs proceed to England for demobilization	
	2/2/19		4 " "	
	3/2/19		1 OR admitted to hospital	
	4/2/19		1 LD horse destroyed	
	5/2/19		Capt. Off. Perham R.E. & 3 ORs proceeding to England for demobilization	
	6/2/19		2 ORs proceed to England for demobilization	
	7/2/19		5 ORs " "	
	8/2/19		10 L.D. horses proceeded to BEAUVOIS	
	9/2/19		6 ORs proceeded to England for demobilization	
	10/2/19		5 " "	
	12/2/19		4 " "	
	13/2/19		4 " "	
	14/2/19		8 " "	
	15/2/19		8 " "	
	16/2/19		5 " "	
	19/2/19		5 " "	
	21/2/19		24 LDH & 3 LDM to No 13 V.E.S.	
	22/2/19		4 ORs proceed to England for demobilization	
	23/2/19		1 OR "	
	26/2/19		2 ORs admitted to hospital	
	27/2/19		1 " "	
	28/2/19		1 " "	

Major R.E.
O.C. 92nd Field Coy R.E.

Army Form C. 2118.

WAR DIARY
or
INTELLIGENCE SUMMARY.
(Erase heading not required.)

Sheet No 1.
92nd Field Coy. R.E.
March 1919.

Place	Date	Hour	Summary of Events and Information	Remarks and references to Appendices
I 30 c 7.2	1-3-19. 31-3-19		Coy engaged in constructing XIII Corps I.O.S. CAVDRY. and demolition of 'dud' and 'blind' shells treated by infantry.	
	3/19		1 O.R. reporting from hospital	
	6/19		Major J. Eccles reports up to duty	
			3 O.R.s	
			4 O.R.s proceed to form 219 ¿ ????? Cy R.E	
	7/19		3 " Casualties to hospital	
	10/19		4 " reporting from "	
	13/19		2 "	
	15/19		2 " proceed to Join 219 ¿ ???? Cy R.E.	
	21/19		4 " casualties to hospital	
	24/19		1 "	
			1 "	
	26/19		1 " reporting from hospital	

Army Form C. 2118.

WAR DIARY
or
INTELLIGENCE SUMMARY
(Erase heading not required).

Sheet No. 1
92nd Field Coy R.E.
April 1919.

W.D. 45

Place	Date	Hour	Summary of Events and Information	Remarks and references to Appendices
Sheet 57b. I.30 a 7.2.	1-4-19 15-4-19 16-4-19 30-4-19		Coy. engaged in work as I.C.S. Cavalry. Coy engaged in Camp duties – repair to billets. Checking and cleaning of Eng. stores etc.	Rho
			Casualties	
	1/4 4/4 7/4 10/4 16/4 28/4		1 O.R. admitted to Hospital 3 ORs Evacuated by C.C.S. 3 – Reported from hospital 1 O.R. admitted to – 1 OR reported from – 2 ORs transferred to from 32 Div Sig Coy	

Blunt. 2nd Lieutenant R.E.
O.C. 92nd Field Coy R.E.

O. i/c. 3rd Echelon Details
Balfour House
Finsbury Pavement
LONDON. E.C.

Herewith War Diary of the 92nd Field Company R.E for the month of June, sent to above address in compliance with G.R.O 6978 of the 23/6/19.

2/7/19

R.a. Fitton
Ⅱ Lt. R.E
O.C. 92nd Field Coy. R.E

WAR DIARY
INTELLIGENCE SUMMARY.
(Erase heading not required.)

Army Form C. 2118.
Sheet No. 1
92nd Field Coy. R.E.
JUNE 1919

Place	Date	Hour	Summary of Events and Information	Remarks and references to Appendices
Sheet 57.B. 1.30.a.7.2.	1/6/19 to 18/6/19		Company engaged in finishing the checking of stores & equipment and in Camp duties. All equipment (other than tent in Holland) packed into cases and sacks sealed. All transport and packages given consecutive numbers & described in terms of compliance with Third Area H.Q instructions contained in item O.R. 1561 (Q.A.1) of 7/6/19.	
	19/6/19 to 21/6/19		Company engaged in building two bivouacs in 185th Divisional Packers' area. One at junction LIGNY - CLARY Road (O.10.a.7.5). " " " HAUCOURT - SELVIGNY Road (N.12.d.cent). Preparations for departure of first company.	R.O./J/1 R.O./J/1 II
	22/6/19	06.30	Lt. B. WOOD R.E. with 25 O.R. of Company leaves unit pending demobilisation. Lt. R.A. FITTON R.E. assumes command of Company (Baggage guard) Strength of Company Baggage guard 1 officer & 15 O.R on it's date. (Rest) 0.R. on it's	
	23/6/19 to 30/6/19		Baggage Guard maintains a continuous guard on Company transport and equipment packages.	
			Casualties	
	6/6/19		48780 A/C.S.M. Holland W.H.C. Transferred to C.R.E. AVESNES Sub. Area. 2 O.R. Transferred to C.R.E. ST. QUENTIN Sub. Area. 1 O.R. Reported Evacuated to 5.E. No. 1 Gen Hosp. Leicester.	
	8/6/19			
	1/6/19		T. U. Lt. S.G. GALPIN Transferred to 353 E & M. Coy. R.E. LA FLAQUE in accordance with instructions of C.R.E. No. 3 AREA.	

Sheet No. 2

WAR DIARY
INTELLIGENCE SUMMARY

92nd Field Coy. R.E.

JUNE 1919

Army Form C. 2118.

Place	Date	Hour	Summary of Events and Information	Remarks and references to Appendices
Sheet 57.B I.30.a.7.2.			Casualties (Continued)	
	14/6/19		1 O.R. transferred from 90th Fd. Coy. R.E. awaiting posting after volunteering for extension of service	
	15/6/19		II Lt. J.B. WOOD promoted LIEUTENANT in accordance with provisions of C.D.S. 386 Sect. I (J.) Army form W.3727.	
	19/6/19		1 O.R. (L/Cpl) reverts to Sapper at his own request	
	19/6/19		1 O.R. (Spr) promoted a/L/Cpl with pay from 19/6/19	
	26/6/19		1 O.R. admitted hospital	
	28/6/19		1 O.R. left unit for transfer & disembarkation for demobilization	

R.A. Fulton
Lt. R.E.
O.C. 92nd Field Coy. R.E.

WAR DIARY

INTELLIGENCE SUMMARY. 92nd Field Coy. R.E.
JULY 1919 & AUGUST 1919.

(Erase heading not required.)

Place	Date	Hour	Summary of Events and Information	Remarks and references to Appendices
Shw. 57.B. I.30.a.7.2	1/7/19 to 27/7/19		Company Baggage Guard employed in carrying out a continuous guard over company vehicles and equipment. The vehicles parked in a formation suitable to the purpose. The packages of equipment stored in a locked room in Company Stores. Two more inspections daily by O.C. guard.	Cresswell 3-9-19
	28/7/19		Wagons packed with packages of equipment - checked.	
	29/7/19	09.00 / 11.30	Transport moved to loading ramp at CAUDRY Station. Completed with some instructors in loading operations. Guard left.	
	30/7/19	08.30 / 10.70	Transport loaded on 15 train No. 15 (Serial No. Z.C. 509) by German prisoners. Guard mounted on lire train moved off to DUNKIRK.	
	30/7/19	18.45	Train moved off to DUNKIRK.	
	31/7/19	14.15	Arrival of train at TRIAGE Station DUNKIRK. Guard left. Remainder marched 15 No. 1 N.C.O. & 3 men.	
	1/8/19	08.30	A.M.L.O. notified of arrival of equipment & vehicles.	
	2/8/19	14.30	Vehicles & equipment loaded on 15 barges & receipts given for same.	
	2/8/19	21.20	Baggage guard entrained from DUNKIRK Station for BOULOGNE.	
	3/8/19	02.36	Baggage guard arrived at BOULOGNE (Terlincthun Camp).	R. O. Tilton Lt 92 R.E. W.T.ld O.C.
	3/8/19	10.30	Baggage guard of 12 O.R. handed over 15 Commandant BOULOGNE Dispersal draft camp by O.I/C Baggage guard.	

Casualties - 360409 Spr Pillow J. died of Gas Poisoning W.O.16/19/Rel. P/3748 45735 Dvr Hill W. To R.E. Records Chatham for Discharge 357/Misc/MG18